# Divine Gifts

The Case against Mankind

Dr. 'Abdullaah ibn 'Abd Al-'Aziz Al-Muslih
Secretary-General, Internatioanl. Commission on Scientific Signs in the Quran and Sunnah

O Allaah! To You be praise befitting Your majesty and grand authority. You are The Creator, there being no creator beside You. You are The Provider, there being no provider beside You. You govern the dominion of the heavens and the earth, alone without any partner. You sent to us the best of Your messengers. You revealed upon us the most perfect of Your books. You chose for us Islam as our religion. There is none amongst us but lives beneath the shade of Your blessings and Your signs. Upon us You bestowed minds, which we direct toward Your creation, soundly clarifying to us that everything in existence has a purpose.

Allaah The Almighty Says (what means): *{Have We not made the* earth an expanse and the mountains as pegs? We created you in pairs and We made your sleep for rest.} [Quran 78:6-9]

This could not have happened by chance. There is thus certainly an intent and wise creator. By His mercy, He did not leave creation to their mental variance in knowing the goal of their existence. {Did you then reckon that We merely created you in vain and that you would not return to Us?} [Quran 23:115] Nor did He leave them in disarray when realizing what is of interest to them in both the worldly life and the Hereafter. Instead, He sent to them His finest men, who guided them upon the path, empowering them with clear-cut and certain proofs indicating their truthfulness. The final of those fine men was Muhammad ibn 'Abdullaah, may blessings and peace be upon him and upon his family and Companions. He is the unlettered Prophet for whom an-Nawawi, May Allaah have mercy upon him, enumerated more than 1,200 evidences proving that he is the Messenger of the Lord of the Worlds. To proceed:

Beloved brother and honored sister, it is hoped that Allaah, The All-Hearing and All-Knowing, will benefit you through this article entitled **Divine Gifts: The Case against Mankind**, and that He will Strengthen your faith, Give you insight and guidance, and Provide you with the tranquility of truth and the fortune of attaining it. {Verily in the remembrance of Allaah do hearts find tranquility.} [Quran 13:28]

## Part 1: The blessings, gifts, and favors of Allaah upon His creation:

Man lives in the shade of Allaah's numerous and perfect blessings as he wallows in His expansive favor.

These blessings are too abundant to be counted. To demonstrate the abundance of His blessings, He revealed Surat "An-Nahl" [The Bees], which is also called "an-Ni'am" [The Blessings]. Allaah The Almighty Says (what means): *{If you count the blessing of Allah, you will not reckon it.}* [Quran 16:18]. He also Says (what means): *{They recognize the blessing of Allah, then they deny it, and most of them are ungrateful...}* [Quran 16:83]

**What then are the most manifest of these divine gifts which Allaah bestowed upon His slaves, thereby favoring them, and which none are able to do or give except Allaah?**

### The blessing of an upright creation

**Allaah The Almighty Created the father of mankind, Adam, sallallaahu 'alayhi wa sallam, , with His hands to honor him, and He created him in the best of stature.**

Allaah The Almighty Says (what means): *{Indeed, We have created man in the best of stature.}* [Quran 95:4], and He infused life into him with His spirit. He commanded the angels to prostrate in his honor and with esteem for his offspring, as He The Almighty also Says (what means): *{When your Lord said to the angels, "I am forming a man out of clay, so* when I have completed him and infused life into him with My Spirit, then fall down before him in prostration." All of the angels then prostrated—all together—but not Iblees. He was arrogant and was of the disbelievers. He said, "O Iblees! What prevented you from prostrating for what I have created with My Hands? Are you arrogant or are you of the haughty?"} [Quran: 71-75]

Then to complete the blessing upon man, He created his spouse with whom he could share his solitude. Allaah The Almighty Says about this (what means): *{He is who created you from one soul and made of it its mate, that he may dwell in comfort with her}* until *{they supplicated Allaah their Lord, saying: If You give us one upright, we shall be of the grateful.}* [Quran 7:189]. Al-Qurtubi, May Allaah Have mercy upon him, , the exegete, said in his *Tafseer*:

> The meaning of 'upright' is that he will be a complete child without any deformities.

Allaah The Almighty Says (what means): *{He who created you, then fashioned you, then proportioned you.}* [Quran 82:7], i.e. He made you proportionate with a complete form.

### The blessing of provision and the universe and all it contains being subject to the service of man

Allaah The Almighty put man at the center of worldly authority, having made the world swift to serve him beneficially and continuously throughout his life.

Allaah The Almighty Says (what means): *{He is who created for you all that is in the earth.}* [Quran 2:29]

He also affirmed that whatever is in existence works to serve man. Allaah Says (what means): *{He subdued for you what is in the heavens and what is in the earth; it is all from Him. Verily in that are signs for a people who consider.}* [Quran 45:13] He also Says (what means): *{Do you not see that Allaah subdued for you what is in the heavens and what is in the earth, and He conferred upon you His blessings, apparent and hidden?}* [Quran 31:20]

Allaah then detailed some of these blessings. He Says (what means): *{He created for you livestock, in which is warmth and benefits, and from which you eat. There is beauty in them for you, as you drive and as you graze. They bear your heavy loads to a land you would not reach except through great difficulty. Verily your Lord is truly kind and merciful. He created horses, mules and donkeys for you to ride and as adornment, and He creates what you do not know.}* [Quran 16:5-8]

Allaah then Says (what means): *{He is who sent down water from the sky, from which you drink, and from which come trees on which you graze. Thereby He causes for you the growth of crops, olives, date-palms, grapes, and all kinds of produce. Verily in that is surely a sign for a people who reflect. He subdued for you the night and the day and the sun and the moon, and the stars are subdued by His command. Verily in that are surely signs for a people who intellectualize. He also subdued what He created for you in the earth of different colors. Verily in that is surely a sign for a people who remember. He is who subdued the sea that you may eat tender meat from it, and that you may take out of it* ornaments that you wear. You see the ships plowing through it. He subdued it that you may seek of His bounty and that you may give thanks.} [Quran 16:10-14] He also Says (what means): {Allaah is who created the heavens and the earth. He sent down water from the sky, bringing thereby produce as your provision. He subdued for you the ships that they may course through the sea at His command. He subdued the rivers for you. He subdued for you the sun and the moon, both being constant, and He subdued for you the night and the day. He has given you all that you asked of Him. If you count the blessing of Allah, you will not reckon it. Verily man is truly unjust and ungrateful.} [Quran 14:32-34]

Look then, my dear brother and sister, at the blessings outlined in these passages from the book of Allaah. Look how these blessings expressed in the first passage started with the creation of the universe and everything that is in it for the sake of mankind. You can thus see the extent of the Creator's concern for all people. The purpose of creating animals was then explained; that they were created for the benefit of man: for consumption, clothing, warmth, riding, carrying loads, and as beauty to behold. Then the discussion turned to the descent of rain, that man may drink thereof, and then its benefit to the growth of trees upon which animals graze and from which various fruits are borne. All of that is for the sake of mankind. Then came the creation of seas and rivers, which ships course through to transport Allaah's blessings of goods and provision to mankind, and in which are fish with tender meat and pearls to adorn. The passage ended by speaking about a great honor that Allaah conferred upon man, that He gives him all that he asks Him of. The exegete Jamaal Ad-Din Al-Qaasimi, may Allaah have mercy upon him, said in *Mahaasin at-Ta'weel*:

> *{He has given you all that you asked of Him}:* i.e. all that you need in order to amend your conditions and livelihoods, as you asked or requested of Him implicitly without naming them.

## The blessing of guidance by embedding (necessary) precedents and uncontested facts in the mind:

**Ever since he was created, man has not ceased to wonder: Where do I come from and where am I going?**

Many are the answers given by different schools and philosophies, being just as Allaah The Almighty Says (what means): *{Each party exults in what they have.}* [Quran 30:32] The minds were confused as they wondered: who has absolute, self-evident, and necessary knowledge which man is unable to do without? The truth is one, not many. Allaah Says (what means): *{That then is Allaah your Lord: the truth. What then is after truth except delusion? Whence then are you turned away?}* [Quran 10:32]

The principle of non-contradiction (negation and affirmation cannot coincide) is one of these necessary innate axioms which Allaah embedded in the human mind to guide it to the truth.

Nations, old and new, have agreed that man's existence came from

Allaah, The Living Maker who Manages the universe, mankind and life. One group, however, alleged that nature produced man by chance. Their first contradiction is seen by Arabic speakers, as the word for nature, *tabee'ah*, is a passive participle meaning something "created", thus requiring an active participle, i.e. a "creator". [Translator's note: The same could be said in English for "nature", from Latin *natura*, "birth", from *natus*, "born", which requires a "bearer".] The word itself confirms the existence of The Creator The Almighty. As such, their claim that nature is the active source of everything is baseless. Allaah Says in refutation of some pre-Islamic Arabs who held this opinion (what means): *{They say, "There is not but our present life. We die, we live, and nothing causes us to perish except the passage of time." They have no knowledge of that. They are only guessing.}* [Quran 45:24], i.e. their opinion is delusional and baseless. He The Almighty Says (what means): *{They have no knowledge of it. They only follow assumption. Verily assumption suffices nothing of the truth.}* [Quran 53:28] That is because the fundamentals of beliefs can only be built upon certitude, not on mere possibility and illusion.

Moreover, mankind is more advanced and has more freedom than nature. We go into space and dive into the depths of the seas, while nature is subdued, restricted, and bound to its own laws.

May Allah have mercy upon the poet of Islam, Muhammad Iqbal (d. 1938), who addressed the atheist advocate of his time, Karl Marx (d. 1883), by saying:

> *How far the orbits are from you, for you are free,*
> *while they are but compelled as they return and flee.*

Allaah The Almighty Indicates this truth, Saying (what means): *{Indeed We have honored the children of Adam; We carried them through land and sea; We provided them of the good things; We favored them with preference over many of whom We created.}* [Quran 17:70]

Furthermore, nature is deaf and dumb, careless whether man is guided toward the truth or away from it. Thus, the opinion that nature haphazardly created the living world is to give credence to the idea that if ink was spilled on the ground, it would eventually produce a grammatically correct and eloquently written book free of error (referring to the Mus-haf), while the ink itself has no knowledgeable writer behind it.

The renowned Muslim scholar Ibn Taymiyyah, May Allaah have mercy upon him, said in *Dar' Ta'aarudh al-'Aql wan-Naql*:

> It is unacceptable that man's desposition and formation be the result of a "nature" that lacks intelligence and will, as mankind was made with far more order and wisdom than those seen in the construction of homes and the production of spectacular crowns worn by kings.

He also said:

> It is known that the transformation of semen into a human or a beast is a greater wonder than silver transforming into a ring, or wood into a bed or a door, or yarn into a woven garment.

An intelligent poet realized this and said:

*Could you reckon the articulate mind*

*an invention of nature dumbfounded?*

We see the magnificence of a blossom's symmetry, the beauty of an eye's artistry, the harmony in the arrangement of teeth, the delicate system of blood vessels and nerves, the extraordinary design of the human cell, and so forth of what we see in the world of human anatomy.

The Yemeni prominent scholar Muhammad ibn Ibraaheem al-Wazeer (d. 840 A.H) said in *Īthaar Al-Haqq 'Alal-Khalq* (1/48):

> "If it was possible that such as this could exist without a maker, it should be that there are constructed homes, written books, knitted garments, and fashioned jewelry without builders, writers, weavers or jewelers."

The Noble Quran explained this particular naturalist fallacy. Allaah The Almighty Says (what means): *{In the earth are neighboring tracts, vineyards, crops, and date-palms sharing a single root system and otherwise, watered with one water. We favor some over others regarding fruition. Verily in that are surely signs for a people who intellectualize.}* [Quran 13:4]

Mansoor As-Sam'aani (d. 489 A.H), an exegete of the noble Quran, said in his *Tafseer*:

> In this verse there is a refutation against the advocates of "nature", as the same water, soil and heat produce fruits that are different in color and taste ... and it is impossible that a single nature produces two different things.

This line of reasoning was also reflected by the most renowned exegete of the Quran Al-Qurtubi, who said in his *Tafseer*:

> The Saying of Allaah The Almighty (which means): {*watered with one water*} ... is the greatest proof for the invalidity of naturalism. If nature was the doer in making such things with water and soil, there would be no variation.

Rather, *variation* is a certain indication that the Maker and Creator is the one administrating and managing these varieties united by a single essence, yet varying quite differently in color, taste and benefit. Such wisdom shows that behind the scene is one Wise and Intent, Cognizant and Acquainted: Allaah, The Living and Sustaining—not nature inanimate.

Botanists have demonstrated this, explaining how plants are nourished through capillary *action*. The plant takes the specific nutrients it needs and leaves what it does not. This has been explained by what is called the process of natural selection. It can thus be said to a naturalist: Natural "selection" means there is a choice, and a choice requires an intent and decisive intellect, so does the plant have intellect or does "nature" perceive what it does?

Nature is a dumb, deaf and blind idol which has been deified by this materialistic culture since the day religion was put aside. So, faith in nature and faith in idols are much the same, as both are faith in something inanimate, unable to reward for good or to punish for evil. This is a veil over reality and denial of the Hereafter, when reckoning and retribution will take place. The oppressor is thus now in a better and more fortunate state than the oppressed.

Is this the right way to seek the truth, O human mind!? If you did justice, you would say: I was unable to restrain my desire, so I covered the truth while believing in my heart, or due to some doubt I had about the truth, and my ignorance prevented me from knowing how to dismiss it.

Allaah The Almighty Tells us about idols, Saying (what means): *{Do they have feet by which they walk, or hands by which they strike, or eyes by which they see, or ears by which they hear? Say: Summon your partners, then plot against me and give me no respite. Verily my ally is Allaah, who revealed the book, and he is allied with the righteous.}* [Quran 7:195-196]

They wanted to make of this deaf and dumb "nature" a god with an action , while it is merely an idol that collapsed under the gavel of clear cut, certain, and intuitive proof brought by Islam. We shall present this proof for the people of this age, which is plagued by this superficial idea for which there is no evidence save mere illusiion.

## Part 2: Proofs of faith and establishing argument against mankind

In order to establish the wholeness of blessing, the perfection of grace, the guidance of creation to The Creator, and in order to know the goal for which man was created upon this earth: the mercy of Allaah established for him sure proofs, manifest signs, and a conclusive argument, that he may know the path

**connecting him to Allaah The Almighty, as indeed Allaah Demanded that he populate the earth.**

Allaah The Almighty Says (what means): *{He brought you forth from the earth and sought that you inhabit it.}* [Quran 11:61], i.e. He Obliged you to populate the earth, which is only done through establishing justice and civilized construction, bringing harmony between the material society and between religion, moral values, ideals, mercy, and love among mankind. As such, the only choice left for man in this world is Allaah or ruin: either the course of Allaah that results in all goodness and the benefit of humanity as a whole, or deviation that contributes to man's demise, which is what we have witnessed throughout the history of man's existence on the face of the earth.

## The first proof: Innate sense (Fitrah)

**Fitrah linguistically means:** The state of something at the onset of its existence. **According to Sharee'ah terminology, it means:** The innate knowledge about Allaah which mankind was provided with.

Abu al-Haytham said: The Fitrah is the design upon which the fetus was formed in the belly of his mother; as in the words of Allaah, quoting Ibraaheem ('as) *{except who 'fatara-ni', then surely He will guide me}* means: "formed me".

Our Messenger, sallallaahu 'alayhi wa sallam, uncovered this matter for us, saying, *"Every babe is born upon the Fitrah, then his parents make him a Jew, Magus or Christian."* [Al-Bukhaari and Muslim]

The Fitrah is thus the basis of formation. This is a truth in which Muslims believe, as Allaah created man as something pure and clean, believing in the existence of a living creator who raises and maintains him. When he happens to deviate, it is due to outside influences instigated by whims and desires, like the love of one's ancestors and their traditions; or due to doubts. If man follows faith, he then follows the Fitrah upon which Allaah formed him. But if he follows something else, his path will be at odds with this Fitrah. Faith in Allaah is thus implanted in the depths of the human psyche. This internal sense of Allaah's existence is a type of evidence firmly set in the cells of which man is comprised. Further to this point, even the corrupted Fitrah is quickly revived when a person is faced with hardships; actually, whenever the affliction or disability tightens, certainty in Allaah is even more abundant and firm. Allaah The Almighty Says (what means): *{If harm touches you, unto Him your voices rise.}* [Quran 16:53] and: *{If harm touches you at* sea, astray go those whom you call except Him; then when He delivers you to land, you turn away; and man is ungrateful.}* [Quran 17:67] Knowledge gained in times of need is more firmly-rooted than the product of thought in times of free will.

As such, knowing Allaah does not require intellectual evidence or theoretic proof. The Fitrah itself, by necessity, testifies of the wise maker.

Thus, we find that the believer lives in an equilibrium between spiritual demands and corporeal needs, between the basis of his design, and between his behavior, legislation and living. The likes of this accord, harmony and consistency are only found beneath the shade of Islam.

If then we look at the life of a Muslim, we find that it is happy, sociable and tranquil. It is much different from the life of a non-Muslim, characterized by having split personalities, lacking harmony between body and soul, and lacking equilibrium between the Fitrah and its outside influences.

This is why we believe that all people were born upon the Fitrah, which is the first gift given to us by Allaah, proving His existence. In reality, all people believe in Allaah through their Fitrah, as the knowledge of His existence is set in their souls. Even the non-believer recognizes this, but he covers the truth. This is the meaning of disbelief in Arabic: *kufr*, i.e. "covering". The cause of this cover comes from desire—and it is said that "sins lead to kufr"—or from suspicions which are adorned by the devils of men and Jinn alike. Allaah The Almighty Says (what means): *{Who whispers into the hearts of men; of the Jinn and of men.}* [Quran 114:5-6]

Scholars of Islam have said that the causes of man's mistakes are four: greed, envy, anger and desire. It was reported that the Caliph 'Umar ibn Al-Khattab, may Allaah be Pleased with him, said to his governors, "Do not strike the Muslims as to humiliate them, and do not restrict their rights as to make them non-believers." [Ahmad, *al-Musnad*, 1/384/286]

Restricting another's right to a dignified life and what it entails, of food, clothing, shelter, marriage, or medical treatment, could make him angry, which could lead him to cover the truth out of mere spite.

## The second proof: Mental reflection over Allaah's kingdom

The mind is the highest thing in man. It is the greatest gift Allaah Gave to him and is an incomparable honor. By it he is distinguished from livestock and other animals. The Noble Quran counted the one who neglects to use his senses and mind, not searching for the truth, as one who is more lost than livestock. That is because he does not employ the cognitive tools that were created for him. Instead, he keeps panting in pursuit of his desires and urges. Allaah The Almighty Says (what means): *{Verily the worst of creatures according to Allaah are those deaf and dumb who do not intellectualize.}* [Quran 8:22] He also Says (what means): *{For the Hellfire We have generated a multitude of Jinn and men. They have hearts, but not used to comprehend. They have eyes, but not used to perceive. They have ears, but not used to listen. These are like livestock; rather, they are more astray. These, they are the heedless.}* [Quran 7:179]

The Noble Quran regards the perceptive and reflective mind as a basis for salvation from Hellfire and victory unto Paradise. Allaah Says (what means): *{They say, "If only we had listened or intellectualized, we would not be companions of the Blaze."}* [Quran 67:10]

Islam regards mental preservation as one of the five primary interests that Sharee'ah (Islamic law) seeks to preserve. This preservation is complete, providing protection from doubts, destructive ideas, and vile values that lead to ruin. It also protects the mind from intoxicants and narcotics, as Islam forbade anything that removes one's mental capacity. Even traces of wine that do not intoxicate are forbidden, blocking the means to corruption and as a precaution to the consumption of a small amount becoming a gateway to a large amount. The Prophet, sallallaahu 'alayhi wa sallam, said, *"Whatever intoxicates in a large amount is forbidden in a small amount."* [Ibn Maajah (3393), Abu Dawud (3681), At-Tirmithi (1865), an-Nasa'i (5607)].

Islam seeks to block the paths of the devil and eradicate evil from the mind, out of respect and appreciation for it, in consideration of its role in verifying our responsibility to cultivate the earth, and to establish Allaah's commands which He set for our benefit and prosperity. There are numerous verses in the Qur'an that straightforwardly address the mind, saying that it should look, ponder and search, thus making reflection an Islamic obligation. Allaah The Almighty Says (what means): *{Say: Look at what is in the heavens and the earth, but the signs and warnings do not avail a people who do not believe.}* [Quran 10:101] He The Almighty also Says (what means): *{Those who remember Allaah while standing, sitting, and on their sides; and who reflect over the creation of the heavens and the earth. "Our Lord, You did not create* *this in vain. Glory to You! Protect us from the torment of hellfire."}* [Quran 3:191]

'Abbas Mahmood Al-'Aqqaad (d. 1964), a researcher into matters pertaining to mental usage and reflection, affirmed this in *at-Tafkīr Farīdhah Islāmīyah* (p. 9):

> The obligation of reflection found in the Noble Quran includes all that is contained therein of peculiarities and denotations. It addresses the inspiring mind, the perceptive mind, the wise mind, and the prudent mind, and it does not mention the mind merely in passing. Rather, it discusses this in an intent, detailed manner not found in any other religious scripture.

Due to the importance of the mind in attaining knowledge, a person must ponder the path to the procurement of an education and the attainment of definite beliefs.

Let us analyze the linguistic meaning of the word *'aql* [in Arabic, "mind, intellect"]. The basic derivation of this word, according to some linguists, is that it means restriction and restraint. The scholars of our nation are unanimous that acquiring Sharee'ah knowledge of, looking into, and reflecting over the kingdom of Allaah, along with purifying oneself, complete detachment from carnal bonds, and abandoning desires; will lead man to attaining the truth in a straight way pursuant to the method of the Quran and Sunnah.

The many sciences of the Sharee'ah, coupled with intellectual reflection over the conspicuous blessings and other gifts so copious from our Lord The Most Generous, after abandoning selfish desire, will collectively contribute to gaining insight. One may then discover what

Allaah has Deposited into this vast existence of lessons, signs and blessings, that he may know thereafter that these blessings are a donated gift from Allaah. Then the light of divine knowledge, when it reaches the sound mind, will produce truthful certainty. Employing the mind in this matter is a necessary obligation in the religion of Islam, while the Church fathers regarded the inspired text and the Church itself as the only sources of knowledge. The intellect was discarded. Saint Anselm of Canterbury (d. 1109) said in *Proslogion 1* (translated by Sidney Deane):

> Nor do I seek to understand that I may believe, but I believe that I may understand. For this too I believe, that unless I first believe, I shall not understand.

Paul (d. 67) said in *1 Corinthians 1:19* (with GNT):

> I will destroy the wisdom of the wise and set aside the understanding of the scholars.

As such, the Church waged war against scientists. This fierce war led to the burning at the stake of Giordano Bruno (d. 1600) and to Galileo (d. 1642) being forced in court to recant his idea about heliocentrism (the rotation of the earth around the sun) and to support what the Church considered to be true; that the earth is stationary. Religion and science had clashed.

The mathematician and physicist P.C.W. Davies said in his book *Space and time in the modern universe* that science has distanced itself from the Biblical understanding of cosmogony. However, the Quran and Sunnah have come to dispel the false accusation that religion is incompatible with science. Science, the sound mind, and religion all progress together in harmonious unity. It is not fitting that the mind, given to us by Allaah, should ever be inoperative. Rather, it is a mind's meditation over Allaah's vast kingdom that makes the mindful person, through his reflections, realize that behind this perfect design is something wise; and behind this precision in due measure is the perfection of a powerful producer. If his mind then went on to reflect over the results that he sees, the manifestations of wisdom, graceful artistry, and great planning would become clear. He would know with certain knowledge that behind this wisdom is something intent and judicious. He would know that behind these blessings is something truly generous. He would know that the maintainer of the kingdom of the heavens and the earth is something living and lasting, majestic and great. For that, our Lord The Almighty Commanded us to reflect over His vast dominion. Allaah The Almighty Says (what means): *{Verily in the creation of the heavens and the earth and the difference of night and day, there are signs for those with intellects; those who remember Allaah while standing, sitting, and on their sides; and who reflect over the creation of the heavens and the earth. "Our Lord, You did not create this in vain. Glory to You! Protect us from the torment of Hellfire."}* [Quran 3:190-191]

The man confused by the various paths may ask about the true method of using the mind to prove the existence of The Creator, so we say to him: The correct method and safest, most marked, and fairest path is the method of the noble Quran. Allaah Condensed therein this greatest of theorems, using the clearest intellectual proofs, called [evidence of invention] by the scholars of Islam. Allaah The Almighty Says (what means): *{Or were they created from nothing? Or are they the creators?}* [Quran 52:35], and then He challenged them, Saying (what means): *{Or did they create the heavens and the earth? Rather, they are not certain.}* [Quran 52:36]

The summary of this Quranic method, of which our Lord Told us, can be summed up in three sure axioms:

**The first axiom** is that every deed requires a doer. This is one of the most intuitive intellectual postulates. Man is a creature on earth, and he came to exist after his non-existence. Allaah The Almighty rhetorically Asks Saying (what means): *{Has there ever been an instance in time for man when he was not something mentioned?}* [Quran 76:1]

He also Says (what means): *{How do you disbelieve in Allaah, while you were lifeless and He made you live?}* [Quran 2:28] It is not possible for a person to contend with this and to claim the existence of a product without a producer to produce it. This theorem is innate, intuitive and indisputable, as intellects old and new have agreed. The alternative is nothing more than acting as a small child; when he is asked about "who broke the glass", he answers in a way as to avoid accusation, suggesting "it broke by itself". You might laugh sarcastically at the invalidity of his response, since the most intuitive of postulates requires that every deed has a doer.

**The second axiom** is that this deed, i.e. creating the complex craft called man, with his incredible composition made in the best of statures, reflects the supreme ability of the wise maker, glory to Him. You can read with your mind and see with the eye of insight and reflection many of the attributes of the doer through his deeds.

For example, the fetus being formed in the mother's womb: From whence comes his food, drink and air? He lives in his mother's belly, feeding from the placenta, and behind three layers of darkness. *{He creates you in the wombs of your mothers, creation after creation, in three layers of darkness.}* [Quran 39:6], i.e. the darkness of the placenta, the darkness of the womb, and the darkness of his mother's belly. Then when he emerges and his provision is cut off with the cutting of the umbilical cord, we find he has new provision in his mother's milk, warm during winter and cool during summer. When he emerges to pur world, we find he has a tongue with which he shouts, declaring his need for nutrition; and two eyes with which he sees; and two feet for walking. All of that is: *{in the best of statures.}* [Quran 95:4]

Insight indicates that the one who brought all of this into being is a great, gracious, and merciful Maker. Through pondering this truth, one can say with complete confidence that such is a truly kind Benefactor. This is seen in the effects of these blessings and this mercy, which encompasses creation from beginning to end. One is then able to say with surety and ease that the One who manifested this is The Cognizant Creator. *{Does not the One who created know, while He is subtle, yet aware?}* [Quran 67:14], as He prepared for man the means to hear, see, speak and move, that he may engage his life in all its phases.

Even in the four ducts of the face: tears in the eye, saliva in the mouth, cerumen in the ear and mucus in the nose, one can realize the far-reaching wisdom in such decent design and correct arrangement.

As such and as one continues his study of human design, he can deduce the attributes of Allaah's perfection; regarding His ability, being the Sustainer of existence, creativity, sovereignity, dominance, perfection of formation of all creatures, wisdom, and knowledge of what is seen and what is unseen. We thus know with certainty that The One who Designed man and Brought him into being is Allaah Alone, without any partner, and that He is described with these great attributes. *{There is nothing like unto Him, and He is hearing and seeing.}* [Quran 42:11]

Why say this and believe this? It is because anything other than Allaah is fake and false, a fallacy to the mind and truth, and a denial of the most intuitive of sure postulates; *{For that is Allaah your Lord the truth; what then is beyond the truth except error?}* [Quran 10:32]

As for the opinion that everything is random, a main reference for those who snub and deny Allaah, then whoever accepts that is thereby betrayed whenever the many manifestations of wisdom in creation reoccur; randomness has no wisdom or permanence, and so rare is its repetition.

Consider a typewriter. If the letters were pressed randomly until a proper word is formed; after a million attempts, it is not likely that the same word would appear. How then could we imagine that such an activity could produce a complete literary work of science? Further, the current library of human knowledge has yet to completely catalog man and the world around him. How right was he who said, "This universe is an immense book and the scholars have merely read some words on its cover."

This universe, with its marvelous design and great constitution, is the loudest speaker against the opinion of randomness and the failure of its claim. As for these, who when asked about what brought the existence of all things into being, they try to hide behind "nature"; and when asked about nature's own design, and that every design must have a designer, and every deed a doer; then they are annoyed when their claims are frustrated by fair researchers of the people of truth and equity. One could say to them: This "nature" was nonexistent before its existence; and something nonexistent does not cause itself to exist. Even your own self, before it existed, was nonexistent. Or did you somehow spontaneously bring about your existence? *{Or did they create the heavens and the earth? Rather, they are not certain.}* [Quran 52:36]

**The third axiom** is that the alleged doer ("nature") is essentially unable to intelligently do anything from beginning to end, being, itself, unaware and inoperative. Ar-Rahaawi, (d. 10c) wrote in *Adab at-Tabīb* (1/35), quoting the Greek philosopher Aristotle (d. 322b):

> "Is it not a wonder that nature, unable to understand, is driven to a designed purpose, yet it does not ponder or reflect over the deed it does?"

Indeed, nature is created, which means it is itself designed, and every creature requires a creator. This is one of those most intuitive postulates, of certainty, fixed in each mind for all mankind.

O seeker of truth! O inquirer for proof! Nothing remains in front of you but to know with certain knowledge which is not mixed with doubt, nor shaken by suspicion, to believe with all confidence that the creator, bestower of blessings, provider, and maintainer of the dominion of the heavens and the earth is Allaah, The Living and The Everlasting, not something other than Allaah. Therefore, He Alone is the generous Lord: loved, served and obeyed. *{Truly to Him belong the creation and the command. Blessed is Allaah, Lord of the worlds.}* [Quran 7:54]

## The third proof: Providence

**Everything in the universe is purposeful, so there must be a wise and intent generator.**

Scientists found that most things they discovered in this world function within a perfectly calculated framework. Such things are directed to the service of man, assisting him in his livelihood to otherwise further him through life.

The first thing that clarifies such providence is found in the design of human organs, formed in agreement and propriety. The teeth do not emerge until the child begins to be independent of his mother's milk, when his need for consuming food becomes obvious. These teeth, in an amazing geometric order, come in as incisors for cutting at the front, followed by the pointy canines, then the wide molars used for grinding food. Saliva then helps to moisten the morsel, with the tongue turning it over as it does so, until it reaches the back of the mouth to be swallowed. When it arrives at the stomach, aided by the liver and gallbladder, different gastric acids are secreted to break the food down into an absorbable substance. This process ends in the intestines, where the beneficial nutrients are transported via the blood to various bodily organs. Once these nutrients reach the liver, they are stored there until the body needs to move, at which time the liver changes some of its store into a sufficient amount of sugar to be discharged into the bloodstream. Finally, the useless remnants end up in the lower torso.

Consider the fingers on the hand. They differ in length, so as to assist in taking hold of things, as they only become equal when grabbing. Fingers of all the same length would make using one's hands very difficult.

Anatomists of old have counted over a thousand benefits to the human organs. Through advancements in science, they came to learn that each cell of the body has its own task aimed at benefiting the person. Joint cells emit synovial fluid to allow movement; eye cells secrete a substance to clean the eye; while microbes attack any foreign body upon its entrance.

Even when the scientists could not find a use for the appendix, they said—based on complete induction—that it must have had some function and some job it performed. They said, for example, that perhaps it was used when man was a vegetarian, before being introduced to meat. Regardless, they affirmed that everything in the human works in the service of man. The same can also be said for the organs in animals.

This providence also appears in many of the laws of the universe. Abu Haamid al-Ghazaali (d. 1111) said in *Ihyā' 'Ulūm ad-Dīn* (4/117):

> Just as none of the parts in your body are useless, thus none of the parts in the cosmos are useless.

The laws of the universe work swiftly over the period of a full year in order to produce food and nourishment for man. If it was not for the movement of the sun and the moon and the coming and going of the four seasons, in which vegetation is produced, then this blessing and great benefit to the continuation of human life would not be accomplished.

Further, the Noble Quran turned attention to the topography of the earth, that its variation in plains, mountains and valleys is also a directed event, being so that man will not stray therein and find hardship in attaining his livelihood. Allaah The Almighty Says (what means): *{He cast* into the earth anchored mountains, lest it shift with you, and rivers and paths that you may be guided.} [Quran 16:15]

Al-Qurtubi said in his *Tafseer* (10/91):

> "Paths" here means: ways and routes you can take through the lands, in order that you do not become confused and stray.

As such, while the intellect follows what it finds on earth of animals, plants, and inanimate objects, it becomes clear to it that everything exists for the benefit of man. Allaah The Almighty Says (what means): *{Livestock He created for you, in which there is warmth and benefits, and from which you eat.}* [Quran 16:5]

In fact, even their hides, fur, wool and hair exist with the goal of benefiting man. Allaah The Almighty Says (what means): *{Allaah has made for you your houses as residence, and He made for you the hides of cattle to be taken as tents, light on the day of departure and the day of dwelling, and their wool, fur and hair as furnishings and temporary provision.}* [Quran 16:80]

Likewise, this providence is shown in the creation of plants, from which man extracts his food, clothing and medicine. Allaah The Almighty Says (what means): *{As a sign for them, there is the dead earth to which We gave life and from which We brought grain, from which they eat. We made therein gardens of date-palms and grapevines, and We caused springs to flow therein; all that they may eat of its produce—and it was not of their own doing. Will they not give thanks?}* [Quran 36:33-35]

But there remain in this universe many things, the purpose of which man has yet to be guided to the knowledge thereof. However, through the process of examination, man sees that everything has a purpose. The Quran confirms this truth, as Allaah The Almighty Says (what means): *{He subdued for you what is in the heavens and what is in the earth; it is all from Him. Verily in that are signs for a people who consider.}* [Quran 45:13]

Based on this, scholars of Islam say that one of the paths to which the Noble Quran calls in establishing the existence of Allaah, is the path of knowing about the attention to detail in man and about the creation of all things for his sake. This path is called *Daleel Al-'Inaayah* [in Arabic, "proof of providence"]. All things in existence correspond to the existence of man. This harmony shows in many animals, plants, inanimate objects, and an abundance of other elements, like rain, rivers, seas, water, air and fire. On a smaller scale, providence appears in human and animal organs, in how they correspond to his life and his existence. This correspondence comes necessarily (i.e. intuitively) from a willful and intent doer, as such could not be by coincidence alone.

**Modern nuclear physics negates the naturalist-materialist theory and proves the existence of Allaah, The Ever-Watchful over the atomic world.**

Philosophers and scientists confirm that everything in this universe is subdued to the service of man, in a way that fulfills all his needs. However, we find the supporters of materialism, like Karl Marx and

Friedrich Engels (d. 1895) and their followers, like Vladimir Lenin (d. 1924), claim to believe in the eternality of inanimate nature; yet they do not acknowledge the eternality of Allaah, The Living Creator who Manages this universe and *{who perfected everything He created.}* [Quran 32:7] The universe, in all its perfection and wisdom, indicates the inevitability of there being one perfect and intent, wise and aware, whose existence is without beginning.

The reason for that returns to the physics of the eighteenth century, that of Isaac Newton (d. 1727). After he discovered the laws of gravity, he sent a famous letter to his friend Richard Bentley (d. 1742), saying to him:

> It is inconceivable that inanimate brute matter should (without the mediation of something else which is not material) operate upon and affect other matter without mutual contact; [...] [t]hat gravity should be innate inherent and essential to matter so that one body may act upon another at a distance through a vacuum [...] is to me so great an absurdity that I believe no man who has in philosophical matters any competent faculty of thinking can ever fall into it.

The physicist Heinz Pagels (d. 1982) explained that classical physics has supported the global viewpoint which is founded on certainty. Accordingly, the laws of nature specify the past and the future in their smallest details; as if the universe was a clock so perfect that no sooner do we know the position of its parts at a certain time, than we would be able to describe the results indefinitely. (Paraphrased)

Usaamah 'Ali Khidhr commented on this, saying:

This philosophy appeared in Einstein's theory of *general relativity*. Despite the revolutionary ideas which this theory presented about the nature of place, time and matter, Einstein considered the heart of the theorem to be founded in determinism, causality, and the subjection of the universe to a set of organized laws. By example, an astronomer is able to predict the times of lunar and solar eclipses, the paths of comets, and so on, simply by applying mathematical formulae.

However, in 1905, materialism was disturbed by Albert Einstein's (d. 1955) theory of *special relativity*. It was the dawn of an understanding most precise and splendid, that material is but one perspective of condensed energy. He formulated the greatest equation in the history of physics: *$e=mc^2$*, or that energy equals the amount of mass multiplied by the speed of light squared.

This confirmed that matter is not a mere solid, as thought by Newton, but that it is an infinite universal reality. Matter is thus flexibly understood, considering that body mass increases with an increase of its velocity. Further confirmation came with a special device called the *particle accelerator*. In 1952, the California Institute of Technology was able to speed up an electron until it reached near the speed of light, causing the mass of the electron to increase nine-hundred times.

Thus came the collapse of materialism. The essence of the universe was then recognized as radiation and energy, not matter. This was followed by the arrival of quantum nuclear physics, or *quantum mechanics*, overturning the understandings of classical physics, toppling the ideas of determinism and causality, and replacing them by probabilities.

British physicist and astronomer James Jeans (d. 1946) said in *Physics and Philosophy* (p. 123), under the heading *The Failures of the Classical Mechanics*:

> But at the other end of the scale there was no success at all; experimental physics was particularly interested in the processes taking place inside the atom, and in this field classical mechanics was failing conspicuously and completely. Perhaps its most spectacular failure was with the fundamental problem of the structure of the atom.
>
> Experimental physics had provided strong reasons for thinking that an atom consists of a collection of electrons—negatively charged particles—together with something which carries just enough positive electricity to counteract the total negative charge of them all—for the total charge on a normal atom is always zero.
>
> Now there is no mechanism within the framework of classical mechanics for endowing such a structure with a permanent unchanging size. Its charges cannot stand at rest, or they begin to fall into one another, and they cannot be in motion or they become a perpetual-motion machine of the kind not permitted by the classical mechanics.

This new physics realized that the mark of symmetry and harmony, in which place and time exist on the cosmic level, completely collapses on the atomic level. Atoms, the fundamental building blocks of the universe, are controlled by physical laws that are radically different from the physics of the cosmos.

Atomic particles move without following the laws of traditional mechanics. They do not move consistently and flowingly from one point to another, but rather by way of intermittent leaps, the paths of which cannot be controlled or predicted. The physicist is thus limited to merely giving probabilities regarding the paths of these particles.

Then came the *uncertainty principle* of Werner Heisenberg (d. 1976), who received a Nobel Prize for this discovery, which dispersed all previous beliefs regarding how mechanics was understood. This principle affirmed that there is an inherent limitation to our knowledge of nuclear laws, showing that determinism and causality both fail in quantum physics.

Heisenberg refuted the principle of unlimited time and energy, as it is in traditional physics, that energy neither ceases nor comes anew; and that it rather only transfers from one state to another. On the nuclear level, there are events that could allow the electron to borrow energy and repay the debt with great speed. In fact, the more energy that is borrowed, the faster the repayment. Therefore, to confirm that the energy is stored, we must first take measurements at two separate yet similar times to be sure that the amount of energy is actually less.

However, the uncertainty principle refuses this confirmation, due to time not being considered uniform on an atomic level. This opens the door to the possibility of a failure, during very minute moments, of the law of *conservation of energy*; meaning that it is possible for energy to appear all of a sudden, then go back to hiding after a short period of time.

Likewise, quantum physics came to inaugurate an understanding, counted as one of the greatest scientific principles without exception, that there is consciousness beyond this universe. This discovery was made by Danish physicist Niels Bohr (d. 1962) whose repeated and highly accurate experiments proved that while no one can measure the contents of an electron, it does behave in the form of probability waves (*wave function*). This wave is spread all throughout space. It is possible that the electron particle could be at any point in that wave at any time. As soon as we are able to observe and measure this, the probability wave, i.e. wave function, collapses and recedes to become a specific point particle.

Heinz Pagels said in his book *The Cosmic Code* that the metaphysical quantum character will remain hidden as long as you are not engaged in discovering new electrons, as its behavior is that of a wave of probability. If you were to look at it, it would—at that moment—be a fixed particle; but as soon as you stop looking at it, it returns to the previous wave-like behavior. This is indeed peculiar and metaphysical. (Paraphrased) Cosmologist and physicist Stephen Hawking (b. 1942) said:

> There must be an entity external to the universe observing it, so that the wave function of the universe collapses and turns into the reality that we witness. Without this observer, this universe will evaporate into a mere test function. (Paraphrased)

Quantum physicist Fred Alan Wolf (b. 1934) said in *Taking the Quantum Leap* (p. 215):

> Consciousness is the creative element in the universe. Without it, nothing would appear.

He also said: But what is this consciousness? It is that element which occurs outside the material world, constricting the wave of probability, thus extracting the expected result. (Paraphrased)

Theoretical physicist Eugene Wigner (d. 1995) explained that when the scope of theoretical physics was broadened to include atomic incidents through quantum mechanics, the concept of consciousness was highlighted again, since it was not possible to establish quantum mechanics laws without resorting to consciousness.

Fritjof Capra (b. 1939), an Austrian-born American physicist and philosopher, said in *The Tao of Physics* (p. 140):

> In atomic physics, we cannot talk about the properties of an object as such. They are only meaningful in the context of the object's interaction with the observer.

James Jeans considered that the universe testifies to the existence of a systematic force that we could call the *mathematical mind*. Astrophysicist Hubert Reeves (d. 1994) said in *Dernières nouvelles du cosmos* (p. 228):

> By necessity or chance, intelligence seems included in the fate of the universe.

Usamah 'Ali Khidhr said:

> When the electronic wave of probability collapses and recedes, the electron will be exposed to observation and surveillance. But who is doing this observing and surveying from outside of the universe, so that things can be revealed as they truly are? It is only Allaah, lofty is His majesty, Creator

of the cosmos. He is the absolute power who brought this universe into existence. There is no escaping this recognition, which is backed by scientific experimentation.

The chemist and astronomer Isaac Asimov (d. 1992) regarded astronomical research as yet to shed light on something that could explain the design of creation based on nature alone.

Atomic research has thus concluded that causality does not control the atom and its laws; and as such, there is infinitely no room to iterate any such "causes". Physical causality failed to explain the existence of the universe. Therefore, since causality is not counted as a controlling factor of the atom and atomic laws, scientists today consider that the whole cosmic design cannot be bound by any causal material law.

## The fourth proof: The dispatch of the Messengers, may Allaah exalt their mention, necessitates the existence of Allaah the dispatcher

From the moment Allaah put mankind on this earth, the revelation of messages did not cease during any age or at any time. The first prophet on the face of the earth was Aadam, may Allaah exalt his mention, and the first Messenger was Nooh, may Allaah exalt his mention, . The sending of the messengers and prophets was successive, so that no nation was left without its own message until Allaah brought it all to a conclusion with their seal, their master, and their leader, Muhammad ibn 'Abdullaah, sallallaahu 'alayhi wa sallam, . This dispatching of messengers was thus a gift from Allaah The Almighty by which He established the proof against creation.

As for those whom the call or message did not reach, then the most preponderant understanding about them is that Allaah shall Test them accordingly on the Day of Judgment. Whoever obeys Him will enter Paradise and whoever disobeys Him will enter the Fire. He clarified this in His Saying (which means): *{On the day the Shin will be unveiled; and they will be called to prostrate but they will not be able.}* [Quran 68:42]

This contains a confirmation from Him of His equity and a negation of injustice, just as He Says (what means): *{We do not punish until We send a messenger.}* [Quran 17:15], i.e. by establishing the case against them through the Messengers and the revelation of books.

It is important here to note that prophethood essentially establishes the existence of the one who sent such a prophet.

If man is left bare of Allaah's guidance, he will be lost in the paths of life. How many thoughts and contradictory opinions surround him! He is undoubtedly affected by these constant external influences which he sees through the behavior of those around him . Add to this all desires and doubtful matters that are beautified to him by the eloquent devils of menankind and Jinn alike. He has none to protect him in his way of knowing the truth, which he is obliged to seek, as he can have no notion of the Knower of the Unseen, to whom he will return, except through the prophets whom Allaah Sent to guide him to what he must believe and to how he must manage his life.

The call of all the prophets was to achieve the full meaning of servitude, in work and worship, is for Allaah  alone. Allaah thus

Dispatched the Messengers to purge the fitrah of faults and to Guide to truth and welfare. Allaah The Almighty Says (what means): *{We did not send before you any Messenger without inspiring unto him that, "There is no god but Me, so worship Me."}* [Quran 21:25]

The word *ilaah* [translated as "god" in the above verse] has over twenty-two meanings in the Arabic language. All of these meanings can be summarized into two definitions. First, that the *ilaah* is the beloved who is surpassed in love by none. Second, that it is the one obeyed above the obedience of any other. These two understandings comprise the true meaning of servitude, about which our Lord Says (what means): *{I did not create jinn and man except to worship Me.}* [Quran 51:56]

When the servant submits his heart, mind, life, conduct and ideas to what his Lord wants, he has freed himself of being servant of anything other than Allaah. This servitude is achieved through submitting to Allaah and excelling in one's deeds with aspirations for His pleasure. This is a right Allaah has over His slaves. Is He not their creator? Is He not their benefactor and provider? Is He not the maintainer of the dominion of the heavens and the earth? Surely it is His right to be the only thing worshiped without partner. This worship is further confirmed in His Saying (which means): *{Say: Verily My prayer, my sacrifice, my life, and my death belong to Allaah, Lord of the worlds.}* [Quran 6:162]; *{my life}* means that the deeds offered in life is itself the worship of Allaah.

Full servitude comprises one's entire life; of beliefs, deeds, manners, and character, and it provides a way to deal with all of life's affairs. Such servitude can only be achieved by obeying Allaah in what He guided us to do for our own benefit. Allaah only Commands the best and only Forbids corruption. He Says (what means): *{Allaah does not like* *corruption.}* [Quran 2:205] This servitude is only realized by truly ridding oneself of being enslaved to devils, to the self and desire, and to the human troops of Satan. Only then is true freedom found and full dignity achieved.

**Supporting the messengers with undefeatable miracles:**

> **Unto every prophet Allaah gave a miracle, supporting him thereby; but what is a miracle; and what is meant by inimitability?**

A miracle is an extraordinary act, coupled with a challenge and the like of which cannot be done by any one.

It is used practically to mean the mode and manner by which Allaah challenged every people to whom He sent a Messenger, that they may know that this Messenger did not bring to them his own arguments for believing in the oneness of Allaah and His rules and His laws; but rather, what he brought was from Allaah Himself The Almighty.

Hence, the miraculousness lies in the challenge itself, as it shows the inability of man to meet this challenge. Such is a sign, proof and evidence that what the prophets and messengers said was indeed from our Lord. Abu Hurayrah, may Allaah be Pleased with him, narrated that the Prophet , sallallaahu 'alayhi wa sallam, said, *"There was no prophet that was not given signs, the likes of which caused men to believe. I was given a revelation revealed unto me by Allaah; and I expect to be the most of them in followers on the Day of Judgment."* [Al-Bukhaari and Muslim]

The greatest miracle of the Prophet, sallallaahu 'alayhi wa sallam, was an intellectual, everlasting and continuous miracle. It is the Noble Quran, which challenged man since times of old until our present day to convene with distinguished men of letters and produce something the like thereof. Allowance was even given for them to bring but ten surahs—forged against Allaah—then further to merely bring a single surah of its like. He The Almighty Says (what means): *{Or do they say that he made it up? Nay, they do not believe. Let them then produce some speech like it, if they are truthful.}* [Quran 53:33-34]

He also Says (what means): *{Or do they say he forged it? Say: Then bring ten forged surahs like it and call upon whomever you can, other than Allaah, if you are truthful.}* [Quran 11:13], and: *{Or do they say he forged it? Say: Then bring a surah like it and call upon whomever you can, other than Allaah, if you are truthful.}* [Quran 10:38], and their situation was just as Allaah Says (what means): *{Indeed they do not consider you a liar, but the tyrants stubbornly reject the signs of Allaah.}* [Quran 6:33]

As for the previous prophets, their miracles were related to the state of their own people. Since sorcery was spread in the time of Fir'awn (Pharaoh), Moosa, may Allaah exalt his mention, brought a stick resembling the product of sorcerers, but it seized what they conjured. No one else was able to do this very thing, so the first to believe in Moosa were the sorcerers themselves, who were the strongest force in Pharaoh's favor.

This sorcery, being a mythical, deceptive and satanic phenomenon, was devoured by a divine and holy reality. These sorcerers were the scholars of sorcery, so they knew with undoubting and certain knowledge that what Moosa brought was *not* sorcery. Rather, it was an inimitable miracle that no human is able to perform. Even when Pharaoh said to them, "I will kill you," they said: *{Decide whatever you decide. You only decide in this life. Indeed we believe in our Lord, that He might forgive us our sins and what you forced us to do of sorcery. Allaah is the best choice and most lasting.}* [Quran 20:72-73] Pharaoh forced them to do something imaginary and founded on falsehood—a mere illusion—but Allaah made what Moosa brought a miracle that overwhelmed the sorcerers, so they were certain that this was from Allaah. Pharaoh himself was also sure it was true, but his soul's desire prevented his confession.

Allaah The Almighty Says (what means): *{They stubbornly rejected them, though their souls were certain thereof, out of injustice and haughtiness.}* [Quran 27:14]

Allaah gave 'Eesa, may Allaah exalt his mention, the ability to revive the dead and to heal the blind and the leper, as his was a time during which medicine had advanced. Allaah The Almighty Says (what means): *{When you shaped of clay the form of a bird by My permission, then blew into it and it became a bird by My permission, and you healed the blind and the leper by My permission, and you brought forth the dead by My permission.}* [Quran 5:110] Allaah Produced these extraordinary events to overwhelm and overtake the material minds turned from the truth brought by the Messengers.

Then when the lights shone for the message of Islam, which was delivered by our master Muhammad, sallallaahu 'alayhi wa sallam, , it came in a time when different aspects of life were in darkness and oppression reigned; tyranny was widespread and religiosity was corrupted. It was a time when Allaah Detested the people of the earth—the Arabs and non-Arabs alike, save a few remaining of people who were following the religion of Ibraaheem—as was narrated by 'Iyaadh ibn Himaar from the Prophet, sallallaahu 'alayhi wa sallam. [Muslim]

At that, Allaah Authorized the mission of our prophet Muhammad, sallallaahu 'alayhi wa sallam, and Gave him more than a single miracle. He gave him many different kinds of miracles. The most apparent and important of these are the six types we will mention below. The message of Allaah's Messenger, sallallaahu 'alayhi wa sallam, was the final, eternal and modern message. If another society comes after this society, able to uncover sciences and technologies surpassing the sciences of today—even thousands of times more—then there would still be in the Book of Allaah and in the Sunnah of His Messenger, sallallaahu 'alayhi wa sallam, overwhelming and startling truths for the minds of men. Allaah shall Present His case in every time period, that the signs of Allaah should remain modern and continuous. Great scientists of the west and the east, specialists in their various sciences, will be defeated and humbled by its magnificence.

These inimitable miracles and guiding evidences came at the hand of an illiterate prophet in an era of ignorance, not in an age of science and discovery. He brought truths consistent with the Fitrah, confirmed by sound minds, and not conflicting with scientific data. Such was affirmed by the French gastroenterologist, Maurice Bucaille (1920-1998) in his book *The Bible, The Quran and Science*.

The evidences for the prophethood of Muhammad, sallallaahu 'alayhi wa sallam, continue, apparent in every age, indicating his truthfulness. Al-Bayhaqi said in the introduction to his *Dalaa'il An-Nubuwwah* (1/19), referring to these evidences:

> If one (evidence of prophethood) was unknown to a group, another would reach them. If one did not work, another would succeed. If one was lost to time, another would remain. In every situation, the proof is overwheliming.

**Different kinds of miracles given to the Prophet, sallallaahu 'alayhi wa sallam, :**

### First: The material miracle

Allaah gave His Prophet Muhammad, sallallaahu 'alayhi wa sallam, many miracles of a tangible and material nature, including:

1) In the Quran: **The splitting of the moon**

Dr. Faruq al-Baz (b. 1938), an Egyptian-American scientist who worked on the Apollo Program, told me that there have been six moon landings made by American astronauts.

Dr. 'Adil 'Abd as-Salam, professor of geography at Damascus University, showed that in an image of the moon brought to earth by the Americans, there appears to be some disruption on the moon's surface, now filled with sand. This region is called the sea of sand. Allaah The Almighty Says (what means): *{The hour drew near and the moon was split.}* [Quran 54:1-2]

Anas ibn Malik, may Allaah be pleased with him, narrated that the people of Makkah asked Allaah's Messenger, sallallaahu 'alayhi wa sallam, to show them a sign, so he showed them the moon in two halves, until they saw Mount Hiraa' between them. [Al-Bukhaari]

'Abdullaah ibn Mas'ood, may Allaah be pleased with him, said: While we were with Allaah's Messenger, sallallaahu 'alayhi wa sallam, at Mina, the moon split in two: one part was behind the mountain and the other was in front of it. Allaah's Messenger, sallallaahu 'alayhi wa sallam, then said to us, "Bear witness." [Al-Bukhaari and Muslim]

2) In the Sunnah

Miracles of a material nature found in the prophetic Sunnah include:

**1. Water flowing from between the fingers of the Prophet**, sallallaahu 'alayhi wa sallam,.

This happened more than once and in different locations, being witnessed by many and narrated from such a big number of narrators, which implies conclusive knowledge. The most well-known report is that narrated by Jaabir ibn 'Abdullaah, may Allaah be pleased with him, as he said:

> On the Day of al-Hudaybiyah, the people were suffering from thirst. The Prophet, sallallaahu 'alayhi wa sallam, had a leather vessel in front of him and performed ablution. The people came weeping to him. He asked, *"What is wrong with you?"* They replied, "We have no water to perform ablution or to drink, except what is in front of you." He then placed his hand in the vessel and water began to gush forth from between his fingers, as

> if they were springs, so we drank and performed ablution.
>
> I (Saalim ibn Abi Al-Ja'd) asked him, "How many were there?" He said: "Even if we were a hundred thousand, it would have sufficed us, but we were only fifteen hundred." [Al-Bukhari: 3576]

This is profound proof that Allaah is able to do anything, further showing the Muslim that when he truly puts his trust in Allaah, then Allaah The Almighty will Protect and Preserve him. The gushing of water from between his fingers and its flowing from a small leather vessel is fine, clearcut evidence and plain proof of the truthfulness of this prophet. Such is a token and sure sign that this nation is upon the truth, in which there can be no doubt. This is even more profound than the miracle of Musa, when he struck the stone from which sprang twelve springs, because water quite normally comes forth from cracks in rocks; but it does not pass as such through the flesh and blood of men.

**2. The pining of the palm trunk.**

This was transmitted to us by a group of about twenty Companions of the Prophet, sallallaahu 'alayhi wa sallam, through multiple authentic chains of narration which constitutes conclusive knowledge. Jaabir ibn 'Abdullaah said that:

> On Fridays, the Prophet, sallallaahu 'alayhi wa sallam, would stand, leaning on a palm tree to deliver the sermon. A woman or a man of the Ansaar said, "O Messenger of Allaah! Might we make a pulpit for you?" He replied, *"If you wish."* So they made a pulpit for him. Then when Friday came again and he

went to the pulpit, the palm cried out like a child, so he went down to it and comforted it until its whimpering subsided. He said, *"It is weeping for the loss of what it used to hear of the remembrance."* [Bukhari]

**3. Multiplying food.**

There are many famous stories about this, witnessed by multitudes of people. Jaabir ibn 'Abdullaah narrated that:

> On the Day of the Trench, the Prophet, sallallaahu 'alayhi wa sallam, fed a thousand Companions with only a small amount of barley bread and a single she-kid. [Al-Bukhaari: 4101, 4102]

This was like the miracle of 'Eesa, may Allaah exalt his mention, mentioned in the gospel of *Matthew 14:19-21*:

> He ordered the people to sit down on the grass; then he took the five loaves and the two fish, looked up to heaven, and gave thanks to God. He broke the loaves and gave them to the disciples, and the disciples gave them to the people. [...] The number of men who ate was about five thousand, not counting the women and children.

**4. The praise given by the food itself.**

'Abdullaah ibn Mas'ud said, telling about a time in the presence of the Prophet, sallallaahu 'alayhi wa sallam, , "We could hear the food giving praise while it was being eaten." [Al-Bukhaari: 3579]

There are many other tangible miracles that have been reported from the Messenger of Allaah, sallallaahu 'alayhi wa sallam, , and this is not the time to go into all of them. Rather, they are mentioned in a number of books authored on this specific topic, like *Dalaa'il An-Nubuwwah* by al-Bayhaqi, *Ash-Shifa* by Al-Qaadhi 'Iyaadh, *Al-Khasaa'is al-Kubra* by as-Suyooti, and so forth.

## Second: Unmatchable Eloquence

The inimitable miracle of eloquence is found when the perfect word is conveyed along with the perfect meaning, in such a way that the most eloquent speakers are unable to imitate it, or come up with what is similar to it. The prominent scholar As-Suyuti (in *al-Khasaa'is Al-Kubra*, 1/187) explained that there was none from Quraysh, the tribe of the Prophet, sallallaahu 'alayhi wa sallam,, who even attempted to match its eloquence. Allaah Says in the Quran (what means): *{A book—its verses fortified then detailed—from one wise and aware.}* [Quran 11:1]

Allaah The Almighty Challenged the disbelievers of Quraysh and the other Arabs—rather, even all men and jinn—and no one in existence then would even dare accept this challenge, despite Quraysh, at the time the Quran was revealed, having reached the highest peak of eloquence and oration. Truly, Allaah did Pour the language's beauty and eloquence into the tongue of Quraysh, making them dominant over the Arabs in their markets, where poetic challenges were exchanged, like at 'Ukaath, Thul-Majannah, and Thul-Majaaz.

Therefore, He gave them an open challenge, while they were the most desirous of people to reject and nullify the claim of Muhammad, sallallaahu 'alayhi wa sallam, ; He even Lowered the expectations of this challenge, first by seeking them to produce something wholly like the Quran—for they speak its language and know its meanings—then He

Requested but ten surahs the like thereof. But they were unable. So He Challenged them to bring forth just *one* surah like it. But they could not even try.

Al-Bayhaqi quoted Al-Khattaabi (d. 388 AH) in *Dalaa'il An-Nubuwwah* (1/16) as saying:

> Some scholars have held: That which the chosen one, sallallaahu 'alayhi wa sallam, presented to the Arabs of speech, that which disabled them to produce something the likes thereof, is more amazing a sign and more apparent an indication of truth than raising the dead and healing the blind and leprous, because it came to the folk of fluency, the lords of language, the masters of eloquence, those advanced in linguistics. Yet this was a speech, the meaning of which was clearly understood to them. Their disability is even more amazing than the disability of one who watched Christ raise the dead, because they were never before able to do that; or healing the blind and the leper, as they had no knowledge of treating these illnesses. But Quraysh were given this fluency, eloquence, and oratory skill, so being unable to even attempt matching it truly indicates the knowledge behind his message and the truth behind his prophethood. This is a clear-cut case and a plain proof.

This miracle of the Prophet, sallallaahu 'alayhi wa sallam, conveys more perfectly than the miracles of those prophets who preceded. The previous prophets challenged their peoples with things they fundamentally could not do. As for the Prophet Muhammad, sallallaahu 'alayhi wa sallam, , he challenged a superbly eloquent people regarding their own speech and the eloquence thereof; but they could not respond. Furthermore, those who saw the miracles of the other prophets have died, so these miracles only remain in their reports—and hearing is not like seeing. The miracle of Muhammad, sallallaahu 'alayhi wa sallam, is different. His challenge to all Arab laureates, throughout the ages, to produce but a single Surah, remains for all people in every time and in every place—yet none are able to compete. Allaah Says (what means): *{If you are in doubt about what We revealed upon Our slave, then bring a surah of its like and call upon your witnesses, other than Allah, if you are truthful.}* [Quran 2:23] So He even gave them respite to seek help from the people of fluency and eloquence!

> Al-Bayhaqi said in *Dalaa'il An-Nubūwah* (1/12):
>
>> This evidence concludes that he could not have told the Arabs to bring something like it if they are able, while he claimed that they would never be able, unless he was truly certain that they would not be able. It is not possible that he could have had this certainty unless he was thus inspired by his Lord, being given His word.

As truly Allaah Says (what means): *{Then if you do not do so, and you will never do so.}* [Quran 2:24] Further, from another perspective, Allaah revealed that which their hearts concealed, making clear to His prophet, sallallaahu 'alayhi wa sallam, that they actually knew this was true and that it is impossible to be an invention of man; and that nothing prevented them from recognizing his prophethood except arrogance, envy and stubbornness. He Says (what means): *{Indeed they do not consider you a liar, but the tyrants stubbornly reject the signs of Allaah.}* [Quran 6:33] This was the case with Abu Jahl. It is reported in *Al-*

*Maghaazi* (1/27) by al-Waaqidi and by at-Tabarani in *al-Mu'jam Al-Kabeer* (24/346/860) that Abu Jahl commented on the dream of 'Aatikah bint 'Abd Al-Muttalib, saying to Al-'Abbas, may Allaah be Pleased with him:

> We and you are like two horses on a bet. We competed in glory for some time. Then, when the riders came parallel, you say, "We have a prophet!" All that remains is for you to say, "We have a prophetess!"

Despite the disbelief of Quraysh and their opposition, their masters and chiefs would eavesdrop at night, listening to the recitation of Allaah's Messenger , sallallaahu 'alayhi wa sallam, out of amazement, bewilderment and perplexity at the splendor and beauty of this Quran. Ibn Hisham reported in his *Seerah* (1/315) that:

> Abu Sufyaan ibn Harb, Abu Jahl ibn Hishaam, and Al-Akhnas ibn Shariq […] all went out one night to listen to the Messenger of Allaah, sallallaahu 'alayhi wa sallam, while he was praying in his home. Each of them took a seat, listening intently, not knowing the place of one another. They spent all night listening, until the dawn broke and they departed. They met on the road and found fault with each other for what they did. It was said, "Do not return to this, for if some of the fool among us saw us, something undesirable might enter their souls." They split up until the second night, when they all returned to their same places, listening all night until the dawn broke again. They left and then met again on the road, so it was said, "We should not depart until we all make a pact

that we will not return again." So they made a pact upon that and then went their separate ways.

This was due to the clarity of the Quran, the beauty of its style, and the high level of its language. It thus affected them greatly and they were unable to oppose such eloquence, except through combat and oppression. Rather, their avoidance of the truth was out of arrogance and conceit. Look at the case of 'Utbah—Abu al-Waleed—ibn Rabee'ah when Quraysh sent him to the Prophet, sallallaahu 'alayhi wa sallam, to demand that he stop insulting their gods and to curb his call, until he even offered him some spoils in the process. When he finished speaking, the Messenger of Allaah, sallallaahu 'alayhi wa sallam, said, having listened to his speech, *"Have you finished, Abu al-Walid?"* He replied, "Yes." He said, *"Then will you listen to me?"* He said, "I will." The Prophet, sallallaahu 'alayhi wa sallam, then recited to him: *{Ha. Mim. A revelation from the gracious, the merciful; a book—its verses detailed—as an Arabic recital for a people who know; heralding and warning, but most of them turn away so they will not hear. They have said, "Our hearts are sheltered from that to which you call us. We are deaf to it. There is a veil between us and you. Work what you will, for we are also working." Say: I am only a mortal man like you. It has been inspired unto me that your god is one god, so go straight to Him and seek His forgiveness. Woe then to the partner-makers, those who do not give the poor-due (zakaah), and the afterlife they deny. Verily those who believe and work righteous deeds, for them is a reward uninterrupted. Say: Will you indeed disbelieve in He who created the earth in two days and will you make others equal to Him? That is the Lord of the worlds. He made therein mountains towering above. He blessed it and proportioned its sustenance in four days—for those who* *ask. Then He turned to the heaven while it was as smoke, then said to it and to the earth, "Come both, willingly or by force." They said, "We come willingly!" He completed them as seven heavens in two days, and He inspired into each heaven its command. We have adorned the nearest heaven with lamps and protection. That is the measure of the mighty, the knowing. But if they turn away, then say: I have warned you of a scourge like the scourge of 'Aad and Thamood.}* [Quran 41:1-13]

Ibn Hisham narrated this in his *Sīrah* (1/294), and then continued:

> Then 'Utbah went to his companions. Some of them said to each other, "We swear by Allaah that Abu al-Walid returned with a face different than when he left." When he sat with them, they said, "What is behind you, Abu al-Walid?" He said, "Behind me is that I have heard a word—by Allaah!—I have never heard the like thereof. By Allaah!—it is not poetry, it is not sorcery, and it is not fortune-telling."

He was overwhelmed and overtaken by the beauty and splendor of this clear speech. He even warned Quraysh to leave Muhammad, sallallaahu 'alayhi wa sallam, alone, but they would not listen due only to their arrogance and false pride.

NB: The translator has skipped a part of the source text for the reasons which he mentions in his comment on the skipped part.

**Third: The Miracle of Guidance**

This kind of miracle is the goal and greater objective of the Noble Quran. Everything else is but a means to this end.

Allaah the Almighty Says (what means): *{Verily this Quran guides unto that which is straightest, and heralds the believers who do good works that to them belongs a great reward.}* [Quran 17:9], and the Noble Quran has also taught us that Allaah has given man various levels of guidance:

1. Innate direction, which is the guidance given to man and beast alike, to their interests that are essential for maintaining their lives. Allaah The Almighty Says (what means): *{Glorify the name of your Lord the most high, who created then proportionated, and who destined then guided.}* [Quran 87:1-3] So Allaah Proportioned man, Perfected his creation then Destined for him the ways leading to his living, and then Guided him to them. Education is also such guidance.

2. The guidance of success, inspiration, and firmness upon the truth. Thus man was created with the nature of seeking knowledge. Of men are those who are free of the external influences of blind obedience to tradition and holding to the customs of tribe and race. They love searching for the truth so they can be guided to it. However, desires of temptation restrict their reaching that guidance. AllaahCommanded us to ask Him for guidance and for firmness upon the truth and to not let our wants betray us. We repeat this in our five daily prayers, reciting (what means): *{Guide us to the straight path, the path of those upon whom You blessed; not of those with whom You are angered, nor of those astray.}* [Quran 1:6-7] This rank of guidance is special to whomever Allaah wishes of His slaves. He Says (what means): *{Indeed, you do not guide whom you like, but Allaah guides whomever He wills; and He is most knowledgeable about those guided.}* [Quran 28:56]

He thus forbade such guidance for His prophet's own uncle, while he was the closest of people to him, as he fell under the pressure of his tribe, saying, "I fear shame and disgrace." Yet, He provided this guidance to those distant in lineage, like Salman the Persian, Bilal the Abyssinian, and others of His excellent servants.

As corruption, tyranny, and darkness overtook the world, Islam came to illumine it with its light, streaming into the hearts and minds, thus liberating them and raising their level of awareness; so they abandoned everything other than Allaah.

Due to this purpose and this gallant goal, the Messenger of Allaah, sallallaahu 'alayhi wa sallam, went forth conveying the religion of Allaah to the world, spreading it therein, and befittingly striving in His way. The Companions and the righteous Muslims after them spent their blood and wealth to carry this religion to the corners of the civilized world, even when faced with sure torment. They suffered terrible sufferings in order to preserve it for themselves and for those after them. There are many cases of this. By way of example, in China there are villages on mountaintops, in which people live in austerity to hold on to their religion. As for Islam, on the surface of the Tibetan Plateau—between Pakistan, Balochistan and China—there are such villages established in the mountains. These people are saying, "We live in dire straits, but we safeguard our religion." Likewise, Russia went to war with Islam without showing any leniency, and no one can imagine the extent thereof, but Islam remained and could not be concluded.

In Russia, I have seen with my own eye and have heard with my own ear, when I visited for a seminar on the scientific miracles of which I now speak. In this conference convened at the Gorbachev Foundation, which was once the site of an institute for spreading atheism throughout the world, the president of the foundation said, "We used to export "There is no god" to the world; then you came to confirm to us, in the language of science, that "There is no god but Allaah".

At the conclusion of this conference on scientific miracles, seven major Russian scientists embraced Islam, merely on the dismissal of atheist claims. Muslims have thus emerged from the shadows, from the middle of the fire, saying, "There is no god but Allaah, we are Muslims, and our faith will not be seized."

That and many other eyewitness accounts indicate that Islam is truly Allaah's religion, which agrees with the Fitrah; and that it is not possible for anyone to whom its power and influence has reached to remove that guidance from the hearts and instincts of men. This is the miracle of guidance that, when coupled with a sound heart, remains therein and clings thereto. Allaah Says (what means): *{They want to extinguish the light of Allaah with their mouths, but Allaah completes His light—no matter if hated by the disbelievers.}* [Quran 61:8], and: *{Those who disbelieve spend their wealth to avert others from the way of Allah; so they will spend, then they will regret, and then they will be defeated.}* [Quran 8:36]

The greatest witness borne to verify this religion as the religion of human nature is that Islam never entered a land and then left it. Instead, it took residence, continued therein, and became part of its essence. The only exception to this would be Al-Andalus, which the Muslims abandoned for a wisdom known only to Allaah and as a lesson for whoever takes heed. They apparently left for two reasons, which are the plague of nations: disputed leadership and desired extravagance. Those with insight should learn this lesson well.

This was Spain, in which the infamous courts of the Inquisition were established in order to bring an end to Islam and the Muslims. But despite that, the testimony of the Islamic civilization's lasting effects stands until our present day, bearing witness that Islam is the religion of science.

### Fourth: The Legislative Miracle

The illiterate prophet Muhammad ibn 'Abd Allah, sallallaahu 'alayhi wa sallam, brought a system of law that occupies a moderate place among contemporary positive systems of law. He brought welfare that supports the poor person until he attains the first degree of self-sufficiency, guaranteeing what is required by necessity, not by luxury and opulence.

Regarding the amount of *Zakaah* to be paid to the needy and the poor, an-Nawawi said in *al-Majmoo'* (6/193):

> They are given whatever takes them out of need and puts them into self-sufficiency, so that they will remain sufficed. This is reported verbatim from Ash-Shaafi'i and has been supported by the narration of Qabeesah [...] that Allaah's Messenger, sallallaahu 'alayhi wa sallam, said, *"Asking others' financial help is not allowed except in one of three cases... and a man who is stricken by poverty and three men of wisdom among his people acknowledge that, he may ask until his living is sufficed."* [Muslim: 1044]

He also said (6/191):

> What our opinion entails is that the person finds full sufficiency in food, dress, shelter, and all other necessities, according to what befits his condition with neither extravagance nor parsimony, whether for himself or against the one who invested in him.

Ibn Rushd said in *Bidaayat al-Mujtahid* (2/39):

> How much must be given? [...] Al-Layth [ibn Sa'd] said, "He is given what is used to pay for a servant, if he has a family and the Zakaah money is plentiful." [...] Most have agreed that [...] he is given money until he reaches the first stage of self-sufficiency.

Then if the given amount of Zakaah is insufficient, they are to be provided for by any surplus wealth kept for the common welfare; but if the treasury's budget is unable, then sufficiency for the poor is requested to be given by the wealthy. The scholar al-Juwayni said:

> All Muslims have agreed that in the case of a time in which there are impoverished and humiliated poor, it is obligatory upon all people of wealth and ease to strive in helping these people toward sufficiency.

Ibn Hazm mentioned in *al-Muhalla* (4/281/725) that there are many evidences for this from the Book, the Sunnah, and the sayings of the Companions. We will be sufficed by mentioning one of these evidences here. Allaah The Almighty Says (what means): *{It is not righteous to turn your faces east and west, but righteous is the one who believes in Allaah, the last day, the angels, the Book, and the prophets, and gives wealth—while loving it—to his relatives, the orphans, the poor,* *the traveler, those who ask, and for emancipation; and establishes the prayer and pays Zakaah.}* [Quran 2:177]

Al-Qurtubi said in his *Tafseer* (2/241):

> His Saying (what means): *{and gives wealth—while loving it}* is used as evidence by those who say that there is a right to wealth beside Zakaah. [...] I say that the meaning of the narration transmitted on this topic is verified by this verse itself, since He Says (what means): *{and establishes the prayer and pays the poor-due}*, mentioning the poor-due, indicating the intended meaning behind *{and gives wealth—while loving it}* is not the poor-due tax. That would be redundant.

The legislative miracle of the Noble Quran appears in the obligation of settling a debt on behalf of the impoverished debtor, using the general welfare treasury (Bayt Al-Maal)—if the country has wealth—and such legislation was unknown to positive laws throughout the entire world, even until today. Allaah Says (what means): **{The Prophet is more closely allied to the believers than their ownselves, and his wives are their mothers.}** [Quran 33:6]

Abu Hurayrah narrated that the Prophet, sallallaahu 'alayhi wa sallam, said, when Allaah Granted him victories, *"I am more closely allied to the believers than their ownselves, so whoever has died of the believers and left a debt, I must settle it; and whoever left wealth, it will be given to his heirs."* [Al-Bukhaari: 2298, Muslim: 1619]Another narration has: *"...if he did not leave its payment, we must settle it."* [Al-Bukhaari: 6731]

It was also narrated by Ja'far as-Saadiq from his father, from Jaabir, with the wording: *"Whoever left a debt or those bereaved, then such is unto and upon me."* [Muslim: 867]

Abu 'Ubayd said in *al-Amwāl* (1/282/543):

> That he considered they had this right after death, such is considered even more during life.

Al-Munaawi said in *Faydh al-Qadeer* (2/171):

> His saying *"then such is unto and upon me"* means that the issue of taking care of his dependants goes "unto me" and the settling of his debt is "upon me."

Al-Qurtubi said in his *Tafseer* (14/122):

> Some scholars have said that the ruler must utilize the treasury to settle the debt of the needy, following the example of the Prophet, sallallaahu 'alayhi wa sallam, , when he announced his obligation to do so by saying, *"I must settle it."*

Islam also recognizes the public ownership of natural resources, like minerals and petroleum—even if it is found on private property, according to the preponderant opinion of the Maaliki school, and this is the opinion about petroleum alone according to the Hanbali school. The same is said for the national ownership of conquered lands. The Caliph 'Umar ibn al-Khattab, may Allaah be Pleased with him, dedicated the lands of the Levant (Ash-Shaam), 'Iraq, and Egypt to all generations of the nation—while maintaining the right to individual ownership—citing the obligation of the wealthy to replenish the treasury for the common welfare and to suffice the nation's needy.

I attended a conference on Islamic economics in Baden, Germany. Present were at least 110 Muslim economists and 120 economists from Western Europe, who came to debate the economic policies of Islam. One major western economist stood and delivered a final statement, in which he said, "It is clear to me and to my colleagues that the world's salvation from its economic disaster is what you Muslims have presented."

In early March 2009, the official Vatican newspaper *L'Osservatore Romano* published an article by Loretta Napoleoni, in which she stated that "the ethical principles on which Islamic finance is based may bring banks closer to their clients and to the true spirit which should mark every financial service."

As for this miracle in the field of healthcare, one member of the British House of Commons spoke during a session regarding the spread of AIDS, which has become the main focus of many people, and the House asked her opinion on solving the problems presented by this world-threatening disease. She said that the solution to the AIDS disease is the Saudi solution. By "Saudi", she meant "Islamic", i.e. punishing whoever commits a sin in which AIDS is contracted, thus cutting off the phenomenon of AIDS itself.

There are many other perspectives of the legislative miracle, like in criminal justice, trade and business, family ties, and foreign affairs. Even the United Nations considers the Islamic Shari'ah as one of its references.

Unfortunately, this is not the place for expanding on all of these points. The sources for such can be found in books of jurisprudence, politics, and other books related to the system of human life according to the laws and rulings of Islam.

### Fifth: The Miracle of the Unseen

Ibn Taymiyyah said in *Sharh al-'Aqeedah al-Asfahaaniyyah* (1/202):

> Of the prerequisites to prophethood, is that there must be some foretelling of the unseen, told to the prophet by Allaah The Almighty. If he does not tell of the unseen, he is not a prophet.

There have been about a thousand reports from the Prophet, sallallaahu 'alayhi wa sallam, telling of the unseen. The judge 'Abd Ar-Rahman Al-'Eeji said in *al-Mawaaqif fi 'Ilm al-Kalaam* (1/356), enumerating the ways to prove the Prophet's, sallallaahu 'alayhi wa sallam, truthful claim to prophethood:

> Seventh: His foretelling of the unseen. This is found in the Quran and in the authentic narrations. Whoever looks into this will find many such evidences.

Abu al-'Ala' al-Qushayri composed a book, called *Ma fil-Quran min Dalaa'il an-Nubuwwah*, regarding what is found in the Quran of such proofs of prophethood.

In the Surah entitled *Al-Fat-h* [The victory], there are a number of obvious statements of the unseen, like the promise of conquering Khaybar to the people of al-Hudaybiyah—to the exclusion of all other people—then the promise fulfilling the Prophet's, sallallaahu 'alayhi wa sallam, dream that they would perform 'Umrah in Makkah while the Quraysh are still there, and the promise of those Beouins who did not witness the treaty of al-Hudaybiyah, along with the promise of their future victories against a people of great military force, and the promise that Islam will conquer the eastern and western horizons of the earth. All such prophecies came true.

Muhammad Wali Allaah An-Nadwi composed a book entitled *Nuboo'aat ar-Rasūl*, written for his master's degree, and in which he mentioned 186 true prophecies, not including the six he conveyed with weak chains of narration. He said, "I only mentioned them because they came true."

Regarding the Islamic conquests, Ibn Khaldoon said in his *Taareekh* (1/375):

> Their capture of Persian and Roman lands, three or four years after the passing of the Prophet, sallallaahu 'alayhi wa sallam, was one of his miracles [...] and such miracles cannot be compared to normal occurrences.

Many scholars have written books entitled *Dalaa'il an-Nubuwwah* [Evidences of prophethood], the most famous and comprehensive of which was written by al-Bayhaqi in seven volumes. Sa'eed Saalim Baashanfar compiled a book of the same title, in which he collected and mentioned the sources for 1,400 matters of the unseen.

### Sixth: The Scientific Miracle of the Quran and Sunnah

I mentioned in my book *This is Muhammad, the Messenger of Allaah, and these are the Proofs of His Messengerhood* one-hundred contemporary and universally accepted scientific facts, and I mentioned the evidences for these facts in the Quran and the Sunnah. Even when we find a weak chain in some of such narrations of the Sunnah, we can accept—based on complete induction—the benefit therein due to the volume thereof indicating these scientific miracles. There have been many books regarding this written by modern writers.

Since this scientific miracle of the Quran and the Sunnah is a pimary pivot for establishing the proofs and the case against mankind—especially in our present age—we shall examine some accounts thereof in the coming pages of this book.

## The fifth proof: The revelation of Books

Every prophet sent by Allaah was given two things of importance. The first is the Book and the second is the miracle that indicates his truthfulness. These Books contained the laws, manners, rulings, systems, lifestyles, and the method upon which mankind can proceed with Allaah's guidance, which contains directions for their benefit in this life and the next. As Allaah Created them, He Knows what is right for them. Their minds cannot encompass the vast details of what they need, considering that they are often clouded by desires and lustful thoughts. We must believe that Allaah The Almighty is omniscient, knowing the apparent and unapparent—the hidden secrets—of everything. This is not hard to believe, since He is the knowing creator and not a single atom in the universe is hidden from Him. As such, His laws, commandments and instructions for mankind must coincide with what He made of man's fitrah and his corporeal, spiritual, psychological and sociological needs.

No matter how much man learns, he will never encompass all that would benefit him; even if he might have a general knowledge of such—but he will never have knowledge of the unseen, that he might realize its benefit and how to obtain it. Allaah The Almighty Says, quoting the words of His Messnger, (what means): *{If I had knowledge of the unseen, I would have amassed much wealth and never would any harm touch me.}* [Quran 7:188]

Therefore, he is not able to rely solely on what proceeds from sheer intellect. Islamic jurists have said, "The mind should not legislate." This is because the mind, by itself, can only reach certainty about things in the natural sciences, of physics and chemistry and biology and so forth. James Jeans said in *Physics and Philosophy* (p. 140):

> Before the quantum theory appeared, the principle of the uniformity of nature—that like causes produce like effects—had been accepted as a universal and indisputable fact of science. As soon as the atomicity of radiation became established, this principle had to be discarded.

He then said (p. 141):

> In this way we find that the atomicity of radiation destroys the principle of the uniformity of nature, and the phenomena of nature are no longer governed by a causal law.

However, there is no such certainty in human sociology, as even welfare has its positive and negative effects. This is why the poet said:

> *Tell whoever claims—of knowledge—some knowing,*
>
> *"A thing you met, but what of the things forgoing?"*

May Allaah have mercy upon 'Umar ibn Al-Khattab, who delayed any allowances for children until after they were weaned, in order to economize the treasury, but when mothers began weaning their children early, he cried to himself, "O 'Umar! How many burdens you have borne without knowledge?" He then overruled his decision and ordained a hundred dirham for each newborn, then two hundred dirham for a toddler, and then more when he reaches puberty. This instance shows the necessity of adhering to the revelation of Allaah—not personal judgments—as He said the Almighty Says (what means): *{But most people do not know. They know the apparent of the life of this world, but they are heedless of the Hereafter.}* [Quran 30:6-7]

Allaah thus brought to us an inclusive and perfect plan, which secures human well-being by way of His Messages and Books. These books guarantee the well-being of their adherents in their worldy lives and in their lives yet to come. The criteria have been set. These principles preserve presence of mind and bring order to life—and all other matters on an individual, familial, social and national level, in times of peace, war, reconciliation and assistance—and all other affairs of living. He the Almighty Says (what means): *{Allaah knows and you do not know.}* [Quran 2:216]

In the forefront of these affairs, the legislation must be based on believing in the six fundamentals of faith, oft-repeated throughout the Noble Quran: faith in Allaah, His angels, His Books, His Messengers, the last day, and fate, the good and bad thereof. This moreover entails having faith in the unseen, so that a person may realize that there is—at every turn—someone watching. Thereby, he may perfect himself and his work.

After belief, one must work to realize the five practical pillars of Islam, summarized as (1) testifying that there is no god except Allaah, (2) establishing the prayer, (3) paying Zakaah, (4) fasting during Ramadhan, and (5) performing pilgrimage to the House of Allaah if one is able. The goal of these pillars is to train oneself to spend his wealth in good purposes, avoiding avarice and stinginess, in order to eradicate poverty in the nation.

Thereafter, one must affirm the infallibility of the Book of Allaah and the sunnah of His Messenger , sallallaahu 'alayhi wa sallam, accepting them as the only two pure sources of creed and legislation. Then comes the acceptance that the Companions of Allaah's Messenger, sallallaahu 'alayhi wa sallam, were upright and trustworthy, as they were the ones who transmitted this religion and legal system to us. Action must then be taken to establish all obligations of the religion, as indicated by the Book and the Sunnah, whether through direct or indirect evidences. One must also avoid what is forbidden based on such evidences and adhere to the rest of the values, manners, and beneficial regulations thus regulated by the books of Allaah: the highest and most complete of which is the Noble Quran and the purified, authenticated Sunnah.

The sixth proof: The scientific miracle in the Quran and Sunnah

**The significance of the Scientific Miracle is based on several aspects:**

First, we live in a time known as the age of science. There is not a student or specialist, specializing in anything of medicine, engineering, politics, or humanity, except that he says, "We are in the age of science." Young and old are thus involved in this pursuit. It is the criterion for any action or theory. Therefore, it is inescapable that the miracle for our age is a scientific miracle.

Second, the scientific miracle addresses the minds in the best of ways and in the highest levels of comprehension.

Third, the discussion on such a miracle is directed toward those scientists able to understand the intended meanings thereof. The same is said for all those who recognize the importance and scientific worth. The *International Commission on Scientific Signs in Quran and Sunnah* has taken upon itself to put forth this message, to convey it, explain it, and to assemble its standards and criteria for those who work therein.

## Witnesses to the Scientific Miracle in the Qur'an and Sunnah

The witnesses to the scientific miracle found in the Noble Quran and the prophetic Sunnah are many. Scientific experiments and studies published by centers of specialized scientific research have established that these are scientific facts that no fair person can ignore or deny, indicated by great scientists of the west accepting such with esteem, confirmation and amazement.

Prof. E. Marshall Johnson, a major scientist in the field of embryology, once told me, "If the facts corresponded with what the prophets of those in the West brought, the world would stand and never sit. I am amazed at you, though; how can you remain silent while the evidences of the truthfulness of your prophet are clearly right in front of you?"

We will thus demonstrate some of these witnesses to the scientific miracle found in the Quran and Sunnah in the following pages, including some images of this miracle from various disciplines.

### Black Holes

> *{But no! I do swear by the khunnas, the sweepers coursing along; and by the night as it passes and the morning as it breaks: verily it is the word of a noble Messenger.}* [Quran 81:15-19]

**Scientific Evidence**

Black holes represent the geriatric stage in the life of giant stars, five times greater in mass than our sun.

Distinguished by their high density and tight gravitational pull, nothing can escape from a black hole's grip, even light itself (traveling at nearly 300,000 km/s). This reflects the existence of areas, like holes in a page of the sky, everything disappearing therein, so they appear as openings. These giant, vanishing stars sweep away whatever comes in their paths, even stars. This is why some have described black holes as "giant vacuum cleaners". Such was indicated through some theoretical calculations conducted by Karl Schwarzschild (1873-1916) in the year 1916, as well as by Robert Oppenheimer (1904-1967) in the year 1934. Since 1971, support for their existence has increased, and scientists now believe that the center of our own galaxy, the Milky Way, is a supermassive black hole.

**The Miracle:**

Negation before an oath in the Noble Quran is emphatic, as if Allaah The Almighty is saying, "There should be no need to swear having this clear proof already existing." Taking oaths is thus one way to prove that the Quran is a revelation from Allaah. He The Almighty Says (what means): *{But no! I do swear by the khunnas, the sweepers coursing along; and by the night as it passes and the morning as it breaks: verily it is the word of a noble Messenger.}* [Quran 81:15-19]

The enormous importance of an oath manifests itself when considering the object thus sworn as a proof for something greater. Specifically, this oath describes something that shares the attributes of what are called "black holes", which are essentially stars moving along in their orbits, as in the wording "coursing along". As for the word "*khunnas*", its many meanings include: vanishing, veiling, being concealed, receding, and going into oblivion after having flourished.

These are truly giant stars, having passed into their final years, shrinking in mass, hiding away in darkness without any light, but due to the strength of their gravitational pulls, they sweep away whatever crosses their paths, thus increasing their mass and might; they truly are "sweepers", or giant vacuum cleaners.

Knowledge of these characteristics is relatively new, so their appearance in the Noble Quran, in words that describe them with precision, confirms their inspirational value. This is decisive evidence that this is the speech of Allaah The Creator, blessed is He, who Says (what means): *{It is nothing but a reminder to all peoples, and you will come to know the truth of it after some time.}* [Quran 38:88]

{A lamp and a moon giving light}

> Allaah The Almighty Says (what means): *{Blessed is He who has made constellations in the sky, and He made therein a lamp and a moon passing light.}* [Quran 25:61]

**Scientific Evidence**

The energy of the sun, our "cosmic nuclear reactor", comes as the result of combusting hydrogen, its main ingredient, and internally transforming it into helium.

Due to its density, high pressure, and heat reaching 15 million degrees Celsius, there occurs a nuclear reaction and the fusion of four hydrogen atoms into one helium atom. This causes a difference of mass between the initial component and the final product. This in turn causes the emission of electromagnetic energy and the emission of short radioactive waves from the sun's surface in the form of visible, infrared and ultraviolet rays. This means that the sun obtains its energy from within itself through a natural process of nuclear fusion and under conditions of high pressure, density and heat. It is like a giant nuclear reactor used to provide the earth with its light, warmth and energy.

The sun is considered a star. It is a shining celestial body that spontaneously generates power. The moon is more like a planet. It is a fixed celestial body that reflects the light given off by the rays of stars and suns. As such, it functions in the same way as planets.

**The Miracle:**

Over 1,400 years ago, the text of the Noble Quran pointed to the difference between stars and planets, using the example of the sun and the moon.

This realization was reached by modern astronomers after the discovery of telescopes and by applying the studies of photometry and spectrometry to stars and planets in the past few centuries. What is a star if not a shining celestial body that spontaneously generates power? What is a planet if not a fixed celestial body that reflects the light given off by the rays of stars and suns?

The sun is counted as a giant nuclear reactor swimming through space at a great speed. It is light, energy and heat at varying levels and in varying forms. It is not an illuminating disc with a static light. Rather, it is a dazzling lamp *{and We made a dazzling lamp.}* [Quran 78:13]

As for the moon, it is a planet that reflects the light of the sun, thus illuminating the night on earth. The confirmation of this already came in the two previously mentioned noble verses of the Quran. Who then told Muhammad, sallallaahu 'alayhi wa sallam, about these facts? It was only Allaah.

> *{This is a message to mankind, to be warned thereby, and to know that He is only one god; and so that those with perceptive cores may take heed.}* [Quran 14:52]

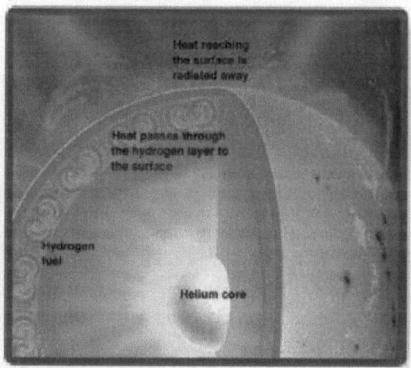

An illustration of the sun's internal core.

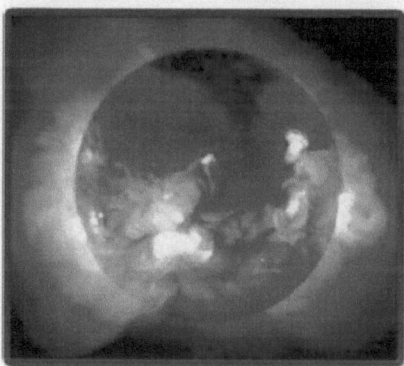

The sun, a blazing lamp generating power.

Air Pressure

Allaah The Almighty Says (what means):

*{Whoever Allaah wants to guide, He opens his breast to Islam. Whoever Allaah wants to leave astray, He makes his breast narrow and confined, as if he is ascending into the sky. As such, Allaah gives torment to those who do not believe.}* (Quran, 6:125)

## Scientific Analysis

Knowledge of the atmosphere's composition remained a mystery until the year 1648, when Blaise Pascal (1623-1662) confirmed that air pressure decreases as the distance above sea level increases.

It later became apparent that air was most concentrated in the lowest levels of the atmosphere. About 50% of atmospheric mass accumulates between 0 to 20,000 feet above sea level. That increases to 90% when it is between 0 to 50,000 feet above sea level. In other words, density will generally decrease with an increase in elevation.

Rarefaction of the air reaches its peak in the upper layers, just before dissipating completely into space.

When man is at an elevation less than 10,000 feet above sea level, there is no serious cause for concern. The respiratory system can acclimatize itself to elevations between 10,000 and 25,000 feet.

But as man rises into the sky, air pressure decreases and oxygen levels decline. This results in a feeling of tightness in the chest and severe difficulty in breathing (dyspnea), as well as a rise in the respiratory rate.

High elevation will also cause irregular breathing due to the sharp decline in oxygen levels (resulting in hypoxia). If he is unable to obtain a sufficient supply of oxygen to his body, his respiratory system will fail, and he will die.

## The Miracle

It is indisputable that mankind, at the time of the revelation of the Quran, knew nothing of the atmosphere's gaseous composition and its various layers. Consequently, a decrease of air pressure in the upper layers and a decline in oxygen levels, to the point of unsustainability, was equally unknown. People were ignorant of the effects this would have on breathing and life, the results of which are respiratory failure and death.

Rather, the opposite belief was prevalent: that the further man ascends, the more open his chest becomes, and that he will only enjoy a more invigorating breeze the higher he goes.

This noble verse clearly indicates two truths only recently affirmed by modern science:

First, that the chest is tightened and breathing is restricted as man ascends through the atmosphere. It is clear that this is caused by a lack of oxygen and a decline in atmospheric air pressure.

Second, that this confinement (ḥaraj in Arabic), which precedes death by suffocation, was relatively recently determined to be at an elevation of 30,000 feet. This is due to a serious decline in air pressure and a dangerous lack of oxygen needed to sustain life, until oxygen is completely absent from both lungs thus leading to man's death.

Without oxygen supply and a special pressurized suit, an astronaut would be unable to stay in space.

Without an oxygen supply and a special pressurized suit, the astronaut would be unable to stay in space.

## The Sky's Return

Allaah The Almighty Says (what means):

*{By the sky, that of return.}* (Quran, 86:11)

**Scientific Analysis**

Modern meteorology has uncovered some of the secrets of the atmosphere and the benefits and protection it presents for the earth. These benefits include:

1. The restoration of water vapor through rain.

2. The remission of meteors, repelling them back into space.

3. The deflection of deadly radiation, pushing it far from the planet.

[Note: All of this restoration, remission, repulsion, deflection, and pushing refer to a single meaning, i.e. causing something to return, just like the act of reflection mentioned below.]

4. The reflection of short and medium wave radio signals back to the earth. One could consider the atmosphere like a mirror, reflecting these rays and electromagnetic waves. It reflects—or causes to return—whatever is broadcast to it, like television and wireless signals, after going through the upper ionosphere. This is the basis of how radio and television broadcasting systems operate throughout the world.

5. The atmosphere also reflects heat. It acts as a protective shield against the sun's heat during the day, just as it works as a cover at night to keep the earth's heat from escaping. Without this balance, life would be impossible on our planet, whether due to extreme heat during the day or extreme chill during the night.

**The Miracle**

The verse {*By the sky, that of return*} indicates that a very important trait of the sky, which encompasses the earth, is found in the process of return.

Forerunning exegetes understood this to refer to rain alone. But modern science has shown a deeper relationship between "return" and the atmosphere. A number of phenomena previously unknown to humankind have been only recently discovered.

The word raj' [translated as "return" in the verse above] can mean "to bring back" or "to return something to its starting point". That is, it means to repel something and to cause it to return in the direction of its source, like an echo.

*{The sky}* here means the lowest heaven, of which the earth's atmosphere is an obvious part. The wording suggests that there should be something of a shield encompassing it, in order to return back every useful thing and to deflect every harmful thing. It has thus been affirmed that the word "return" has implications beyond the mere descent of rain, and that without this trait life would not be sustainable on earth.

The Quran compiled into a single word all that modern science discovered regarding atmospheric peculiarities. Truly great is Allaah, who Says (what means):

*{Say: Praise belongs to Allaah. He will show you His Signs. Then you will recognize them. Your Lord is not heedless of what you do.}* (Quran, 27:93)

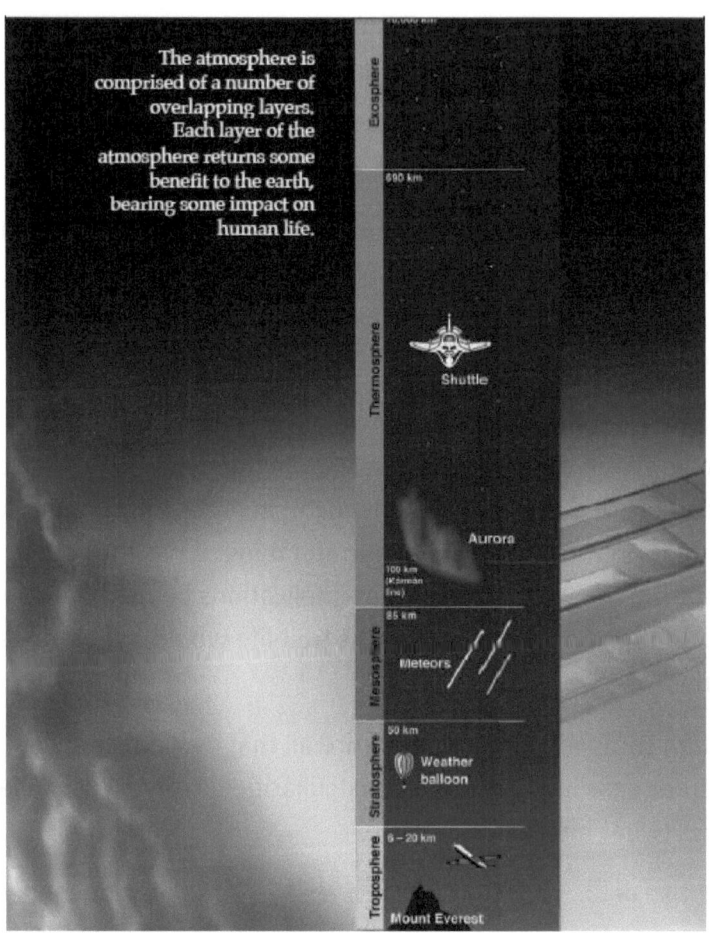

## Nerve Endings in the Skin

Allaah The Almighty Says (what means):

*{Verily those who disbelieved in our Signs, We shall drive them into a Fire. Whenever their skins are roasted through, We shall replace them*

*with new skins, so they may taste the torment. Verily Allaah is mighty and wise.}*

(Quran 4:56)

## Scientific Analysis

The prevalent belief prior to the age of scientific discovery was that the whole body could feel pain. It did not occur to anyone that there were certain nerves that transport sensation and pain to the brain. That was until the role of nerves in the skin was revealed to be so significant, due to the high concentration of nerve endings in the skin.

Sir Henry Head (1861-1940) classified the skin's sensitivity into two groups:

(1) The epicritic, which refers to light sensations, like a tender touch or a slight change in temperature; and,

(2) the protopathic, which refers to the feeling of pain and extreme changes in temperature.

Skin is the primary organ comprising of nerve endings.

Anatomists have shown that a person whose skin is completely burnt away will not feel pain, as his nerve endings have been destroyed. This differs with one who suffers a second degree burn, for example, as his nerve endings are exposed and transmit the pain in all its severity.

## The Miracle

This verse explains that the skin is the part of the body that will feel the punishment. In other words, there must be a connection between the skin and pain.

Furthermore, we are told that once the skin is completely burnt, there will no longer be a feeling of pain. New skin then replaces the dead skin, so that pain can persist and the person who denied Allaah's Signs can be punished in permanence.

Modern science has discovered that the majority of nerve endings are found in the skin. Prior to the invention of the microscope and before advances were made in the study of anatomy, it was beyond anyone's capacity to know about this fact, which was so eloquently presented in the Quran fourteen centuries ago.

This is a certain miracle, showing the dominance of Allaah's Signs in science.

An exteroceptor for the transmission of touch

The Krause end-bulb, thought to be a receptor of cold temperature

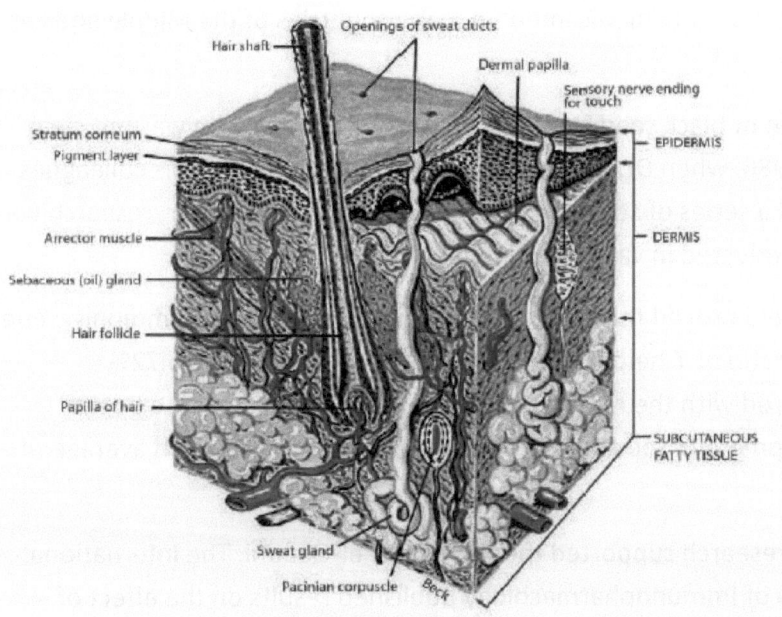

**Black Seed is a cure for all diseases**

The Messenger of Allaah, sallallaahu 'alayhi wa sallam, said,

*"There is no ailment for which there is no cure in the black seed, except death."*

(Al-Bukhaari: 5687, Muslim: 2215)

**Scientific Analysis**

For more than two thousand years, black seed (Nigella sativa) has been used as a natural medicament in many countries of the Middle and Far East.

The role of black seed in enhancing the immune system was not clear until 1986, when Dr. Ahmad al-Qaadhi (1940-2009) and his colleagues started a series of studies in the United States. Thereafter, research was also conducted in various other countries.

Al-Qaadhi proved that the use of black seed strengthens immunity, due to the ratio of T-helper (TH) cells increasing on average to 72% compared with the regulatory T (Treg) cells. There was also noted development in the activity of natural killer (NK) cells to an average of 74%.

Other research supported the findings of al-Qaadhi. The International Journal of Immunopharmacology published results on the effect of black seed on human lymphocytes and polymorphonuclear leukocyte phagocytic activity (August 1995). That journal also published research on the protective effect of black seed oil against murine cytomegalovirus infection (September 2000).

Black seed oil has been tested as an antiviral drug. The acquired immunity was gauged at the earliest onset of infection by limiting the NK cells and macrophages (MΦ) during the process of phagocytosis.

**The Miracle**

The Prophet, sallallaahu 'alayhi wa sallam, told us that black seed is a cure for every disease. The Arabic word shifaa' [cure] was mentioned as an indefinite noun, so the context is general. This means that black seed contributes to the cure of every disease.

It has been scientifically proven that the immune system is the only true line of defense with the ability to combat diseases and produce cells that kill viruses. This includes both humoral and acquired immunity. Specific antibodies can be produced for each individual pathogen, just as specialized killer cells are enabled to fight infection.

Through applied research, black seed has been proven to activate humoral immunity. The research published in scientific journals confirmed this fact. There was an improvement in helper lymphocytes and phagocytes; an increase in interferon (INF) and interleukin (IL) 1 and 2; and a strengthening of cell immunity.

Black seed thus leads to an increase in the system's ability to combat and destroy cancer cells and some viruses. It further helps with scars left by schistosomiasis, or snail fever. Based on the above, we are able to conclude that black seed is indeed a cure from every ailment, because it repairs and strengthens the immune system.

Only a prophet could claim to know these facts fourteen centuries ago. Allaah The Almighty Says (what means): *{He does not speak from desire. It is only revelation revealed.}* (Quran, 53:3-4)

**Joints in the Human Body**

The Messenger of Allaah, sallallaahu 'alayhi wa sallam, said,

*"Indeed every person of the children of Adam was created with three hundred and sixty joints."*

[Muslim: 1007]

## Scientific Analysis

A joint is the junction between two bones or a bone and cartilage or two bodies of cartilage, found anywhere in the human body.

| Total Number of Joints by Area | | | |
|---|---|---|---|
| Head | 86 | Throat | 6 |
| Chest | 66 | Spine and Pelvis | 76 |
| Upper Extremities | 2 x 32 = 64 | Lower Extremities | 2 x 31 = 62 |
| Total = 360 Joints | | | |

The Prophet ☐ said, *"Indeed every person of the children of Aadam was created with three hundred and sixty joints. Whoever exalts Allaah, praises Allaah, declares the oneness of Allaah, glorifies Allaah, seeks forgiveness from Allaah, removes a rock from the road, or removes a thorn or bone from the people's path, commands virtue and forbids vice, to the number of those three hundred and sixty joints, shall walk that day as one who saved himself from the Fire."*

He, sallallaahu 'alayhi wa sallam, also said, *"There are three hundred and sixty joints in a person, so one must give charity for each of these joints."* Those around him asked, "But who is capable of doing that, O Messenger of Allaah?" He said, *"By covering up expectorant if found in the masjid; by removing something harmful from the road; or—if unable to do the others—by praying two units of the ḍuḥā [mid-morning] prayer."* (Ahmad: 22998)

**The Miracle**

The Prophet, sallallaahu 'alayhi wa sallam, mentioned the exact number of joints in the human body—having a total of three hundred and sixty—during a time in which it was impossible to know this number with such precision, as the majority of joints are too small and in places too difficult to define without modern advances in anatomy and histology.

While in agreement with anatomical discoveries of our present age, this knowledge was conveyed by the Prophet, sallallaahu 'alayhi wa sallam, fourteen hundred years ago. He was sure of this claim because the one who told him was none other than the Creator Himself.

{*Does He not know what He created? He is the subtle, the aware.*} (Quran, 67:14)

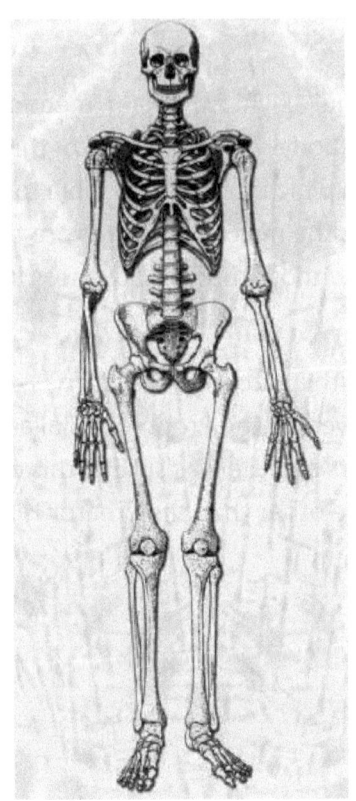

**Sexually Transmitted Diseases**

The Messenger of Allaah, sallallaahu 'alayhi wa sallam, said,

*"No sexual depravity appears among a people to the point of publicity, except that they are plagued by disease the likes of which their predecessors did not witness."*

(Ibn Maajah: 4019)

**Scientific Analysis**

Modern microbiologists have discovered, through the past two centuries, that there are a number of bacteria, fungi and viruses that do not spread except by way of sexual intercourse—including relations between heterosexual and homosexual partners.

If these acts become widespread, the whole society is under the threat of an epidemic such as has never been seen before. That is because the germs will transform until they are incurable by treatment and the body is unable to resist them due to the lack of any defense against them. Likewise, there is an open possibility of the disease mutating further into the future.

These illnesses have come to be known as sexually transmitted diseases; or STDs for short.

**The Miracle**

By way of cause and effect, prophetic guidance has educated us regarding general social practices that could afflict any society.

The cause here is forbidden relations—like fornication and adultery—and homosexual relations that are not criminalized, but rather accepted and popularized.

The effect is the result of sexual promiscuity: the spread of sexually transmitted diseases in an epidemic and destructive way as they will change form in generations to come.

These STDs cause great harm and pain to those afflicted. The world has witnessed sweeping waves spreading syphilis which destroyed the lives of millions. Another STD, gonorrhea, tops the list of infectious diseases, being the most globally widespread of STDs. The latest, most terrifying, and deadliest disease is known as AIDS. Its virus destroys the immune system in humans, wrecking organ after organ in a chain of havoc unknown to man before this time.

This is a clear realization of what the Prophet, sallallaahu 'alayhu wa sallam, warned us about. Such is further evidence to the truthfulness of Muhammad, sallallaahu 'alayhi wa sallam, being the Messenger of Allaah.

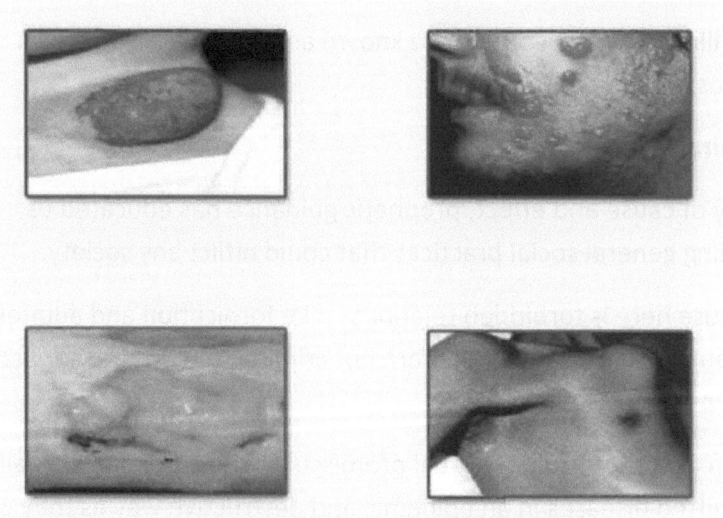

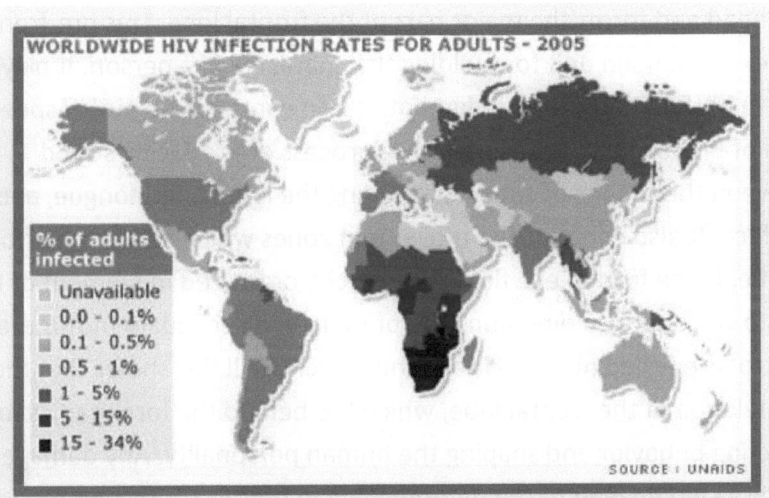

## The Frontal Lobe

Allaah The Almighty Says (what means):

*{Nay! If he does not cease, We shall pull him down by his forelock—a lying, sinful forelock.}*

(Quran, 96:15-16)

**Scientific Analysis**

The human brain consists of four main lobes: (1) the frontal lobe, (2) the occipital lobe, (3) the temporal lobe, and (4) the parietal lobe. Each lobe has its own special function, while at the same time working together and complementing one another.

The frontal lobe in humans is distinctive from that of animals since it includes centers that are responsible for speaking and behavior. It also includes certain neural centers with distinctive functions and places including the pre-frontal cortex which happens to be right behind the forehead and forms the major part of the frontal lobe. This pre-frontal cortex is the main unit for building the character of a person. It plays a role in both initiative and judgment. It also contains the motor speech area of Broca which coordinates the process of producing sound between the organs of speech, including the larynx, the tongue, and the face. It also contains the movement zones which include the frontal eye field. The frontal eye field sustains the organized movement of the eye to the opposite direction. The primary and secondary motor areas control the willed movements of the muscles. All this shows that the frontal area of the frontal lobe, which lies behind the forehead, is for directing behavior and shaping the human personality. Any damage to this area would lead to the deterioration in moral criteria and the efficiency of memory and the ability to work out logical problems.

**The Miracle**

The understanding of this verse was only recently expanded. It is no wonder that the Quran mentioned the area of the forehead as being lying and sinful. Further, the Quran said that this part will be hit and held; this could be an allusion to the area which monitors human behavior. So it is the body part to be held accountable for man's deeds.

It is Allaah's divine wisdom that He Commanded this part to be placed on the ground in prostration so that it will learn how to be honest and upright. Allaah The Almighty Says (what means): *{Prayer prevents lewdness and vice, and the remembrance of Allaah is greater; Allaah knows what you do.}* (Quran, 29: 45)

Human Reproduction

Allaah The Almighty Says (what means):

*{Let man observe that from which he was formed. He was formed from a flowing fluid. It emerges from between the spine and the upper ribs. Verily He is able to return him.}*

(Quran, 86:8)

**Scientific Analysis**

Seminal fluid is a water-based solution containing a great number of sperm. A single sperm cell, called a spermatozoon, resembles nothing less than a drop of water in the macroscopic world; while on a microscopic level, it is an individual spermatozoon that will inseminate the ovum.

The cellular origins of the testes in men and the ovaries in women are located in the backs of parents when they were fetuses. They gather in a common reproductive organ called the Gonad.

Each of them then exits from an area between the spinal column and the ribcage. The ovaries then migrate to the pelvic region by the womb, while the testes migrate to the scrotum, where the temperature is most suitable, otherwise, it will fails to produce sperm at the time of puberty.

**The Miracle**

Regarding His Saying: *{Let man observe that from which he was formed. He was formed from a flowing fluid. It emerges from between the spine and the upper ribs. Verily He is able to return him.}* (Quran, 86:8):

*{Flowing fluid}* is a description of semen, as it is a fluid like water due to the plurality of droplets. However, its components flow and move with excitement. This is affirmed in the Arabic usage of the active participle daafiq for *{flowing}*, indicating its essential movement. All such descriptions are correct when applied to man.

The description in *{it emerges from between the spine and the upper ribs}* clarifies the point of exit for progeny, just as the point of origin is seen in His Saying: *{When your Lord took from the children of Adam, from their backs, their progeny.}* (Quran, 7:172)

He also Says (what means): *{Your sons who are from your spines.}* (Quran, 4:23)

This was not affirmed by science until many wearisome studies were conducted after the invention of the microscope, the crudest of which was invented in 1590 in the Netherlands.

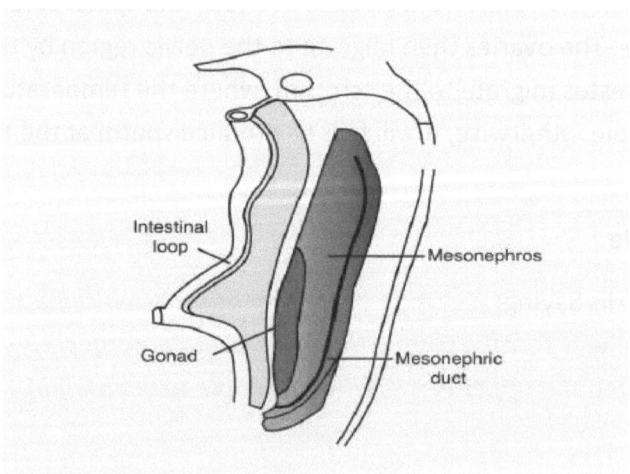

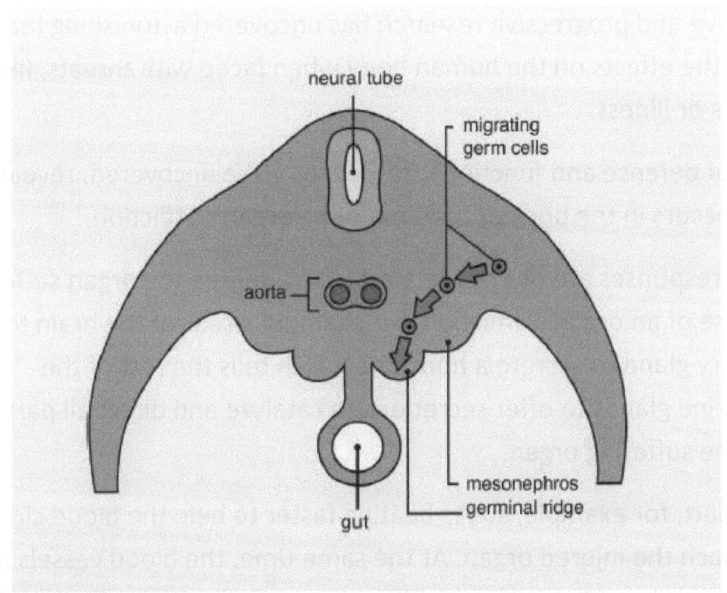

**Bodily Breakdown**

The Messenger of Allaah, sallallaahu 'alayhi wa sallam, said,

*"The parable of the believers, regarding their mutual love, mercy, and sympathy toward one another, is in the likeness of the single body: when one organ suffers, the rest of the body shares in sleeplessness and fever."*

(Al-Bukhaari: 6011, Muslim: 2586)

**Scientific Analysis**

Intensive and progressive research has uncovered astonishing facts about the effects on the human body when faced with threats, like injuries or illness.

Lines of defense and functional responses were uncovered, revealing what occurs in the body at the time of an organ's affliction.

These responses are directly related to the degree the organ suffers. In the case of an organ's affliction, for example, areas of the brain tell the pituitary gland to secrete a hormone which tells the rest of the endocrine glands to offer secretions to catalyze and direct all parts to help the suffering organ.

The heart, for example, starts beating faster to help the blood circulate and reach the injured organ. At the same time, the blood vessels in the inactive body parts contract, while other vessels in the rest of the body expand in order to send the required amounts of energy, oxygen, antibodies, hormones, and amino acids to the injured part. This helps to resist infection and further injury, and in order to heal quickly.

The body starts to break down part of the stored fats and proteins, in order to provide nutrients for the injured organ. This constant sacrifice continues until the rescue is complete, when the injury or disease is under control, and the affected tissues and cells are repaired.

The call from the injured or infected part resembles an actual distress call. The affected area releases pulses to the sensory and alert centers of the brain. Chemicals are released at the first drop of blood shed or when any tissue is torn. Then, all the organs respond, providing help to the affected organ according to the nature of its injury or disease.

**The Miracle**

Prophet Muhammad, sallallaahu 'alayhi wa sallam, explained how the Islamic nation must be regarding its citizens' mutual love, sympathy, and merciful treatment of one another.

He struck an analogy between the single body when one of its organs suffers; that all of it will be affected thereby. There is no word more concise than tadaa'i [translated as "sharing", which is the exegetical understanding, while linguistically it could mean "being in a state of calling one another"] to describe what happens in the body regarding the complaint of one of the organs.

This description came in a short conditional phrase. The condition is the organ's suffering and the response is tadaa'i. This miracle is scientific, linguistic, and rhetorical all at once.

He explained the truth of what happens inside the human body where no eye can observe, using comprehensive words to describe what happens with all of the meanings conveyed in the language, and by way of an analogy that incorporates the meaning into the mind.

Most amazing is that doctors have come to use a name for this part of the autonomic nervous system that reacts to bodily risk and illness that describes the reality of what this system does. It is the sympathetic nervous system (SNS), which comprises the meaning conveyed by the Prophet's, sallallaahu 'alayhi wa sallam, saying about love, mercy, and sympathy.

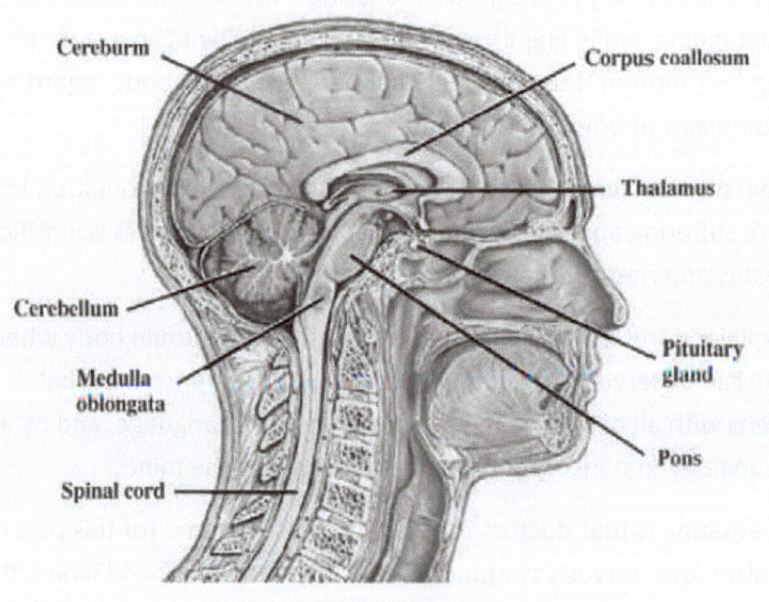

The nervous system acts as an alarm.

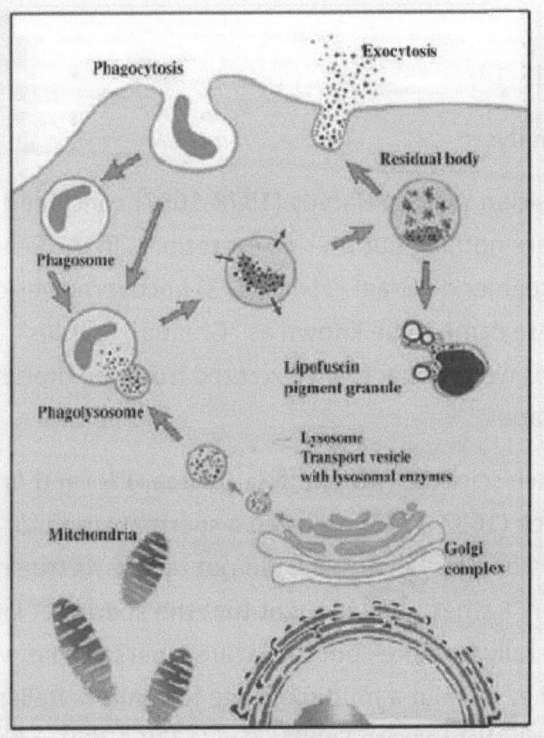

A true battle of cells against foreign invaders.

Embryonic Stages of Development

Allaah The Almighty Says (what means):

*{What is wrong with you that you do not exalt Allaah (as due). While He has formed you in stages?}*

(Quran, 71:13-14)

**Scientific Analysis**

English physician William Harvey (1578-1657) concluded in 1651 that embryos were nothing but uterine excretions. In the year 1672, Dutch anatomist Regnier de Graaf (1641-1673) uncovered vesicles in the ovaries. These came to be known as "Graafian follicles". He concluded that embryos were not actually excreted from the uterus, but instead from the ovaries.

In 1677, Dutch scientists Stephen Hamm (ca. 17c) and Antonie van Leeuwenhoek (1632-1723) revealed a spermatozoon for the first time in human history. However, they did not realize its true role in reproduction. Rather, they thought that the sperm (or later ovum) contained a fully formed—but miniature—person that will grow inside the womb, i.e. without a multiple stage formation. Italian Catholic priest and scientist Lazzaro Spallanzani (1729-1799), who agreed with this theory (called preformation), affirmed the importance of spermatozoa for procreation through his experiments on dogs.

In 1827, about 150 years after the discovery of spermatozoa, Karl Ernst von Baer (1792-1876)—Estonian-Russian biologist—was the first to observe an ovum inside a canine ovarian follicle.

In 1839, Schleiden and Schwann confirmed that the human body consists of basic living structural units and their byproducts. These units came to be known as cells. Thereafter, it became easy to truly understand man's multiple stages of formation. He came from a single fertilized cell, which resulted from the union between a sperm and an egg.

## The Miracle

This noble verse indicates that man is not created all of a sudden, as was the prevalent belief in the West during the century before last and since the time of Aristotle. Rather, it happens during stages of set proportion and includes everyone regardless of racial or generational variance.

The history of embryology testifies to the stumbling of brilliant minds regarding the formation of humans. At the same time, the Noble Quran proclaims—since the seventh century—that man was not made all of a sudden, but rather in proportioned stages, like the construction of a building based on a previous design.

Coincidence cannot explain these proportioned stages, which instead indicate wisdom, intention, capability, comprehensive knowledge, and innovative creation. All of this comes from Allaah. The unity of preparation and planning and the constancy of these stages, regardless of race or generation, clearly point to the oneness of the great creator.

Aristotle's theory that the fetus is formed from menstrual blood continued until the seventeenth century, when the microscopic world was discovered; yet scientists still thought formation was complete without stages.

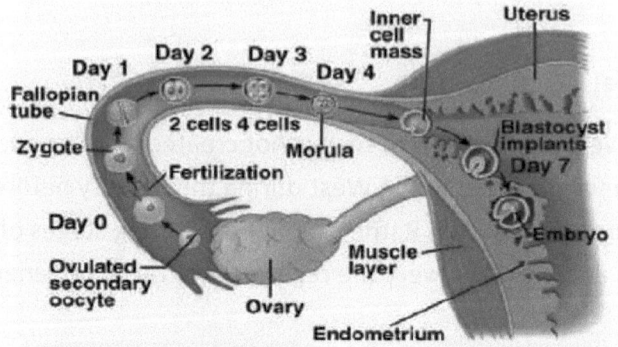

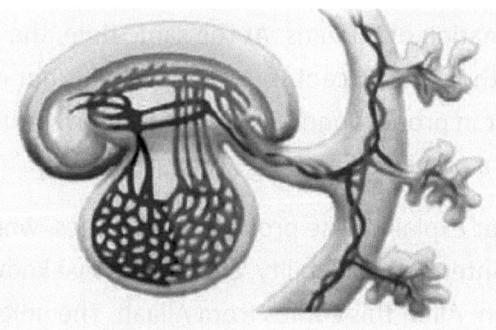

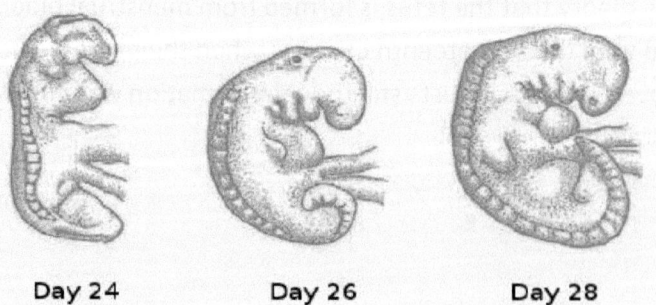

Day 24   Day 26   Day 28

## Quarantine

The Messenger of Allaah, sallallaahu 'alayhi wa sallam, said,

*"If you hear of a plague in a land, do not enter therein. If it befalls a land and you are in it, then do not go out of it."*

(Al-Bukhaari: 5728, Muslim: 2218)

He ☐ also said,

*"The one who flees from the plague is like one who flees from battle, so whoever endures patiently will have the reward of a martyr."*

(Ahmad: 14793, 24527)

### Scientific Analysis

As science advanced, hidden worlds of tiny creatures were revealed, as were the means of their reproduction, spread and their causing of illnesses and epidemics.

It became clear that those who appeared healthy could be carrying microbes of disease and that they were a real source of risk in transmitting the epidemic to other places through travel.

Due to this revelation, a globally recognized and current system of quarantine was developed. It restricts all residents of an afflicted city from leaving, just as it restricts others from entering.

Waves of plague struck Europe in the 15th century until one-fourth of the population was wiped out. Its fury broke off at the borders of the Islamic world. During that period, deadly epidemics and contagious diseases were much fewer in the lands of Islam compared to Europe.

**The Miracle**

Allaah's Messenger, sallallaahu 'alayhi wa sallam, founded a basic principle that only became an essential part of modern preventive medicine after the discovery of germ-causing illnesses and epidemics. This is the principle of quarantine, which prevents the spread of diseases that threaten whole cities and societies.

He, sallallaahu 'alayhi wa sallam, regulated this scientific fact by saying, *"If you hear of a plague in a land, do not enter therein. If it befalls a land and you are in it, then do not go out of it."*

To guarantee the implementation of this great prophetic instruction, the Messenger of Allaah, sallallaahu 'alayhi wa sallam, erected an enclosure around the infected area, and then promised the patient and hopeful, that if they stay put, they will be given the reward of martyrs, while he warned the runaway with ruin and woe. He, sallallaahu 'alayhi wa sallam said, *"The one who flees from the plague is like one who flees from battle. Whoever endures patiently will have the reward of a martyr."* [Ahmad]

Muslims were the only humans who would not flee an epidemic, thus executing the order of their prophet, though not necessarily knowing the wisdom behind it. They became the object of ridicule of nonbelievers due to this behavior, since the healthiest in appearance were considered the most immune. Yet, those who show no outward symptoms while in an infected area are no less likely to be carrying the disease than the visibly ill, as was only discovered in Europe after millions of deaths.

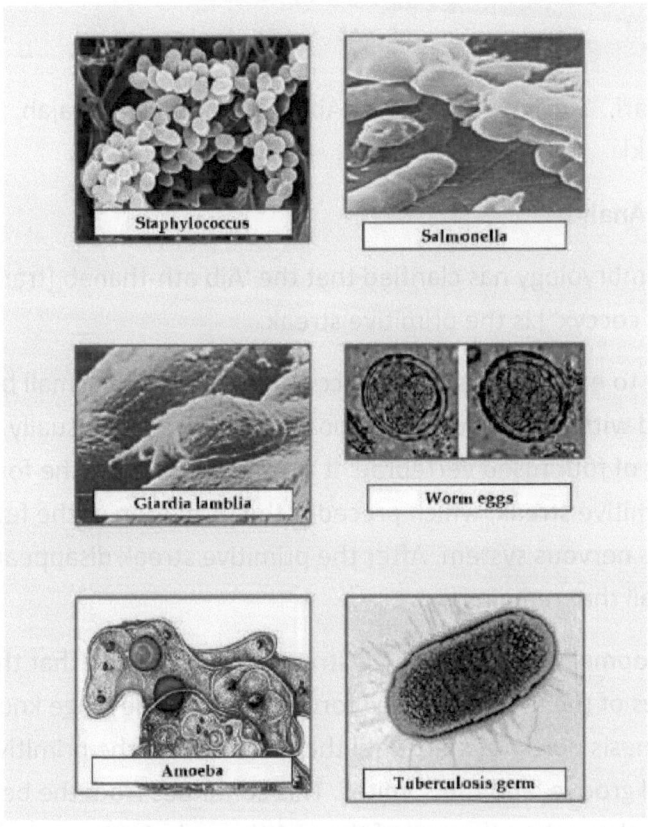

## The Coccyx

The Messenger of Allaah, sallallaahu 'alayhi wa sallam, said,

*"The ground will consume all of the body of the son of Aadam except the coccyx: from it he was formed and in it he will be rebuilt."*

(Al-Bukhaari,, Muslim, An-Nasaa'i, Abu Daawood, Ibn Maajah, Ahmad and Maalik]

### Scientific Analysis

Modern embryology has clarified that the 'Ajb ath-thanab [translated above as "coccyx"] is the primitive streak.

According to embryologists, the coccyx (tailbone) is the small bone associated with the section at the bottom of the spine, usually consisting of four fused vertebrae. It is considered to be the foundation of the primitive streak, which precedes the formation of the fetus, most notably its nervous system. After the primitive streak disappears, the coccyx is all that remains.

The development of the primitive streak is an indication that the organs and tissues of the fetus are being formed. In fact, the stage known as organogenesis does not start until the formation of the primitive streak, the neural groove, and the somites. This continues from the beginning of the fourth week to the end of the eighth week. At the end of this stage, the fetus is equipped with all its basic systems and its organs are formed, followed only by tiny details and bodily growth.

Having fulfilled its purpose in the fourth week, the primitive streak starts to shrink, leaving some traces in the sacrococcygeal region, remaining unseen to the naked eye.

## The Miracle

The narration about the coccyx is a miracle of the Prophet, sallallaahu 'alayhi wa sallam. He basically explained modern embryology, confirming that mankind is something composed and that he originates in the coccyx (or what is called the "primitive streak"). This is where cells are prompted to divide, to take on special roles, and to be distinguished from each other.

Directly after its appearance, the nervous system begins to form; first is the neural groove, then the neural tube, and then the rest of the nervous system. This is the foundation upon which the remaining organs are based. The primitive streak then begins to vanish, leaving but a trace in the sacrococcygeal region, in which the coccyx is formed and from which we will be recompiled on the Day of Resurrection.

*"The ground will consume all of the body of the son of Aadam except the coccyx: from it he was formed and in it he will be rebuilt."*

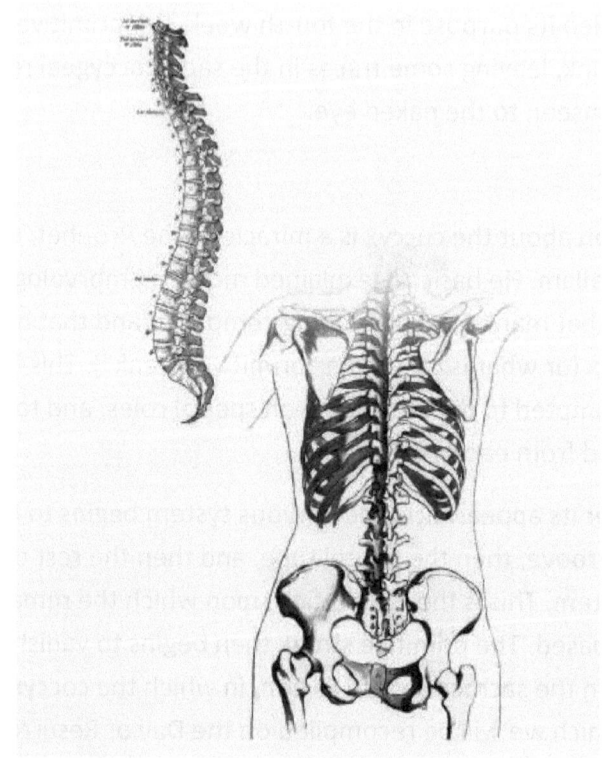

## Pork

Allaah The Almighty Says (what means):

*{Say: I do not find in that which was revealed to me anything forbidden for one to eat, except the dead animal, spilled out blood, the flesh of swine—for that is filth—or an abomination consecrated for other than Allaah. But whoever is forced by need, while not*

*craving or transgressing due limits, then verily your Lord is forgiving and merciful.}*

(Quran, 6:145)

**Scientific Analysis**

Science has come to perceive some points in such things that are deemed prohibited to consume in Islamic legislation which safeguarded its adherents many centuries before the invention of microscopes, and in the same order as in the verse: the dead animal where bacteria grows, then blood where bacteria grows faster especially if there is much blood, and finally swine, in whose body many dangers accumulate and are unresponsive to conventional modes of purification. The body of the young pig is a breeding ground for parasites, bacteria, and viruses that can be easily transmitted to both man and beast. Some of these dangers are specific to swine, like balantidiasis, trichinosis, taeniasis, and cysticercosis, as well as other diseases transmitted between humans and animals, called zoonoses—including various kinds of influenza—and parasites like fasciolopsis and ascaris (causing ascariasis).

Balantidiasis is particularly often found among swine herders and their families, and it spreads as an epidemic, as seen in the 1972 outbreak on the island of Truk in the Pacific Ocean; this was the result of a storm that caused the spread of pig feces throughout the island.

Disease is found wherever pigs are found, even in industrially advanced countries. This counters the claim that it is possible to contain such squalor by way of some modern techniques. We have seen such advanced nations like France, Germany, the Philippines, and Venezuela being susceptible to trichinellosis outbreaks due to the consumption of infected pig muscles.

## The Miracle

Pigs are filthy by nature and feed on impurities. Even the idolaters of old considered it to be a killer of all symbols of good. The ancient Egyptians told the story of how it was a black pig that attacked Horus (their god of protection). The Greek-Canaanite god of beauty, Adonis—as well as the Phrygian consort Attis—was gored to death by a boar.

Swine herders in ancient Egypt were considered to be the lowest of people. They were not allowed entrance into temples nor could they marry outside of their class. Whoever even touched a pig was required to bathe.

According to the belief of the People of the Book, swine flesh is prohibited, even though they do not adhere to such a prohibition. The Quran explained the reason for its prohibition by stating that it is Rijs (An Arabic word that combines the meanings of filth, uncleanness and impurity that carries harm).

The Lowest Point on Earth

Allaah The Almighty Says (what means):

*{Rome is defeated—at the lowest point of the earth—and after their defeat, they shall defeat (their opponent) within a few years.}*

(Quran 30:2-4)

**Scientific Analysis**

Historical records mention that in the year 619, a battle took place between the Persians and Byzantines, who comprised the eastern branch of the Roman Empire. This battle was fought in the vicinity between Daraa and Busra, near the Dead Sea. The Persians won a crushing victory against the Romans, who subsequently suffered gross losses. Contemporaries in that time expected this to be the end of Roman influence in the region.

However, the opposite occurred. In December of 627, a decisive battle took place near Nineveh between the Byzantines and the Persian Empire. The Romans defeated the Persians. After a few short months, the Persians had to resort to ratifying a peace agreement with Byzantium, and the former were forced to return the lands they had taken from the latter.

Geographical illustrations show that the lowest area on the face of the earth is that which surrounds the Dead Sea in Palestine, where it dips lower than 395 meters below sea level. This has been confirmed by geologists and satellite imagery.

**The Miracle**

There are two miraculous points to consider in these noble verses.

First, that which the Quran promised was realized after seven years, as the battle between Persia and Rome concluded in the year 627. The victory of Rome coincided with the victory of the Muslims against the pagans of Quraysh at the Battle of Badr.

Second, a geographical fact was revealed, while not possibly known to anyone at that time. Rome was foretold to lose the battle against Persia in the lowest area of the earth. The word translated here as "lowest" in Arabic is adna, which means both lowest and nearest.

From one perspective, this battle took place in the nearest land to the Arabian Peninsula. From the other perspective, this was the lowest area on the face of the earth according to satellite technology surveying dry land, as mentioned by the Encyclopaedia Britannica.

Historical fact testifies that this battle occurred in the lowest place on the planet, near the Dead Sea Basin. Is this not an indication that the Quran is revealed by Allaah? He Says (what means): *{Say: He who knows the secrets of the heavens and the earth revealed it.}* (Quran, 25:6)

**Earthen Rifts**

Allaah The Almighty Says (what means):

*{By the earth, that of rift.}*

(Quran, 86:12)

**Scientific Analysis**

Geologists have recently discovered that the earth's crust is divided into a network of deep rifts, resulting in twelve main parts called plates, in addition to a number of minor parts called platelets. These plates float over a layer of molten magma, which rises into seabeds and erupts in between two adjacent plates to form new crust.

As one side of a plate increases in size, the other side decreases, while bending beneath the adjacent plate. This shows the existence of what are called mid-oceanic rifts. These rifts cover the earth's crust and can reach a depth of about 150 km, as deep as the crust itself in its thickest place.

Furthermore, all of the continents and their distinct mountain ranges move along with the movement of these plates, making them closer to or further from each other. This is a continuous but slow displacement, being no more than a few centimeters each year. For example, the rift of the Red Sea expands 3 cm annually, while that of the Gulf of California expands 6 cm annually.

Likewise, the colliding of the Indian plate with its adjacent plate caused the creation of the Himalayas, which is home to the highest peaks on the planet.

It is believed today that the current continents were once connected some 200 million years ago, forming Pangaea, a single continent surrounded by a single ocean. The "original" rift, called the Mid-Atlantic Ridge (MAR), is still a region of volcanic activity.

**The Miracle**

Mid-oceanic rifts were not known to scientists until after World War II. Furthermore, they were only explained by the tectonic plate theory after it was formulated in the late 1960s and early 1970s.

On the scientific side, these extended rifts appeared deep beneath the surface of the earth, as landmarks of its crust. The Quran's preceding suggestion to this hidden reality deep underground gives further weight to it truly being the Word of Allaah.

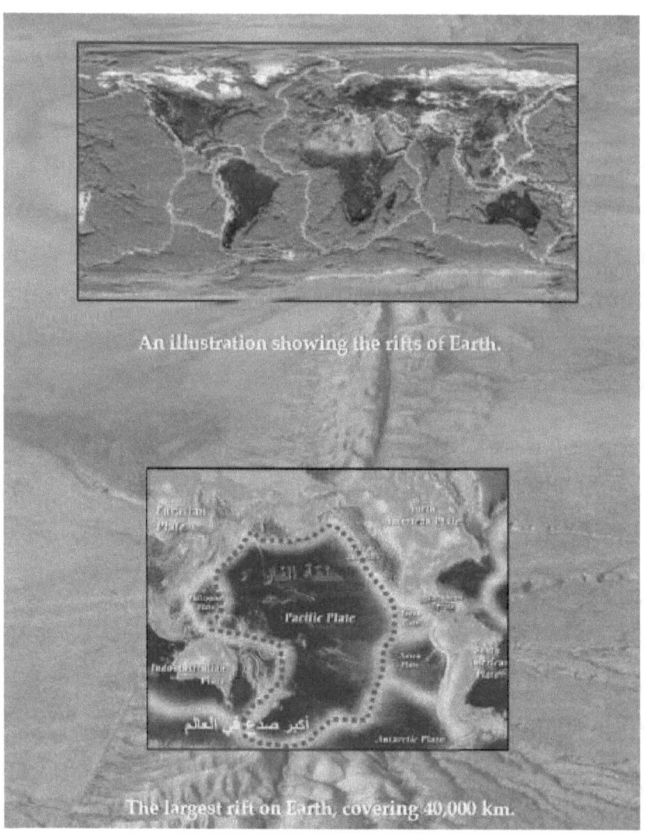

An illustration showing the rifts of Earth.

The largest rift on Earth, covering 40,000 km.

## The Mountains as Pegs

Allaah The Almighty Says (what means):

*{We made the mountains as pegs.}*

(Quran, 78:7)

## Scientific Analysis

Mountains were once thought to be massive piles of rock towering over the earth. That was until 1735, when French geophysicist Pierre Bouguer (1698-1758) noted that the gravitational force in the Andes was much less than expected, considering the apparent size of these "piles of rock". This led him to believe that another part of the rock was buried beneath the earth, thus compensating for the variations in gravity.

In the middle of the nineteenth century, Welsh geographer Sir George Everest (1790-1866) noticed the variation in gravitational measurements between two different spots in the Himalayas. But he was unable to explain this phenomenon, viewing it instead as one of India's mysteries.

Sir George Airy (1801-1892) concluded in 1865 that all mountain chains are masses floating on magma, and that this molten material is denser than the mountains themselves. As a result, the mountains must "plunge" into this high density material to maintain their erect structure.

Geologists discovered that the earth's crust is composed of adjacent continental plates; that massive mountains float along a sea of higher-density molten magma; and that mountains have roots to help them float and to affix them to the plates so the earth will not shake. Geologist Oscar Diedrich Engeln (1880-1965) stated in his book *Geomorphology* (p. 27) that according to the current understanding, each mountain must have its own root beneath the earth's crust.

The principle of hydrostatic equilibrium, regarding the way in which mountains are affixed to the earth's crust, was mentioned in 1889 by Clarence Dutton (1841-1912). He stated that mountains plunge into the earth in accordance with their height. After the existence of plates was proven in 1969, it became clear that mountains maintain the balance for every plate.

**The Miracle**

At the time of man's ignorance about the nature of mountains, which lasted until the mid-nineteenth century, the Quran decisively stated the fact that mountains are like pegs in form and function, driven into the earth. This was only recently confirmed by modern science.

A peg has two parts: the first part is on the surface, while the other is underground, stabilizing whatever is attached to it. Similarly, a mountain has one part protruding from the crust of the earth, while the other is buried deep beneath the ground in accordance with its height. Its function is to stabilize the plates of the earth's crust and prevent them from disarray due to the magma beneath.

This is another indication that the Quran is the Speech of Allaah, The Maker of mountains and universes. He Says (what means): *{He cast into the earth anchored mountains, lest it shake with you, and rivers and paths that you might be guided.}* (Quran, 16:15)

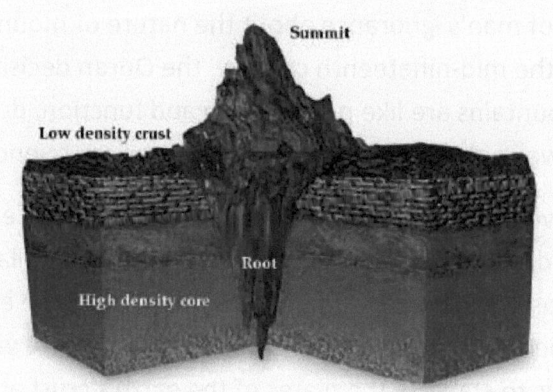

The Merging of Seasand Their Distinction

Allaah The Almighty Says (what means):

*{He merged the two seas. They meet. Between them is a barrier. They do not transgress.}*

(Quran, 55:19-20)

## Scientific Analysis

Seas were not known to comprise of various kinds of water. Instead, the prevalent belief was that each sea had a single nature. This was proven untrue in 1873 by the Challenger expedition (1872-1876).

It was only in 1942 when results came in from various marine research stations, showing that the Atlantic Ocean consisted of waters of varying temperature, density, salinity, habitat, and oxygen absorption.

Such occurs within a single ocean. What then of two different seas? Consider the Mediterranean and the Red Sea, or the Mediterranean and the Atlantic, or the Red Sea and the Gulf of Aden—they all meet at their specific straits.

In 1942, it became known for the first time that seas with varying traits and characteristics merge while maintaining their distinct differences. Even while seas ebb and flow, currents and waves carry water great distances, and hurricanes violently mix what they touch, each unique sea remains intact—as if they actually were separated by some barrier.

**The Miracle**

These verses speak about two adjacent saline seas, merging yet retaining their distinct characteristics, there being a barrier between them, barring one from truly mixing with the other.

Pearls and corals are mentioned in the same passage, indicating that the reference here is specific to bodies of salt water—since such things are only found therein.

Oceans and adjacent saline seas appear to the naked eye as if they are a single mass of water with unified properties. The truth is that they are a collective of bodies with varying values of salinity, temperature and density. This could not have been known without the use of modern technology, yet the Quran precisely mentioned the fact of the matter, explaining the merging and meeting of the seas, along with the barrier that restricts the breakdown of one water into another. Is not that a clear proof that the Quran is the Speech of Allaah.

Allaah The Almighty Says (what means): *{This Quran is not such that it is contrived by anyone other than Allaah. But it is a confirmation of what was before it, and it details the Book—therein is no doubt—from the Lord of the worlds.}* (Quran, 10:37)

## Deep Seas and Layers of Darkness

Allaah The Almighty Says (what means):

*{Or as layers of darkness in an abysmal sea; a wave covers him, above which is another wave, above which are clouds—layer upon layer of darkness—if he were to extend his hand he would barely see it. For whomever Allaah does not give a light, no light shall he have.}*

(Quran, 24:40)

### Scientific Analysis

It is now known that oceans and seas are mostly covered by thick cumulus clouds, as is clearly visible in satellite imagery. These clouds reflect a large portion of the sun's rays, thereby blocking its light.

The remaining light is partially reflected by the surface of the sea, while the rest is absorbed and eventually diminishes into the deep.

There are then levels of darkness in the seas until a depth of about 200 meters, where plant life is unsustainable. At 1,000 meters, there is absolutely no light penetration.

The first device to measure light penetration in water was the Secchi disk, which was invented in 1865 by Italian Catholic priest, Angelo Secchi (1818-1878).

Scientists have been able to observe fish in deep seas—at depths of 600 to 2,700 meters—that use bioluminescent organs to allow them to see through the darkness to catch their prey.

**The Miracle**

This noble verse points to the phenomenon of layers of darkness in deep seas—the term *{an abysmal sea}* means "a deep sea"—and that the darkness in these seas is gradual. The exegete Al-Qurtubi said in his Tafseer (12/275):

It is said that these darknesses are: the darkness of clouds, the darkness of waves, the darkness of night, and the darkness of sea; and that the one who is under these darknesses cannot see anything.

Dense clouds covering the seas reflect a portion of the sun's light. The surface waves then reflect what passes through the clouds. Then, the water absorbs the colors of the solar spectrum, color after color until the entire spectrum is hidden. Finally, internal waves turn the depths into such darkness that if someone stretched out his hand, he would not be able to see it.

The phrase {layer upon layer of darkness} describes the precise reality of what happens in the sea. Just as there are fish at such depths without eyes (as they have no need), there are others with bioluminescent organs, which Allaah Created in order to enlighten their way. This is one perspective of His saying (what means): *{For whomever Allaah does not give a light, no light shall he have.}*

These intriguing scientific facts were mentioned in the Noble Quran over fourteen centuries ago. Who could have told all of this to Muhammad, sallallaahu 'alayhi wa sallam, except Allaah?

**What comes next?**

After these proofs have been presented, perhaps one's heart is given a new life and one's mind is enlightened. Questions may follow, like "What then is the way to Allaah?"

This is the answer:

Allaah commissioned Prophet Muhammad, sallallaahu 'alayhi wa sallam, to convey the right religion and correct method built upon five pillars: (1) testifying that there is no god but Allaah and that Muhammad is the Messenger of Allaah, (2) establishing the prayer, (3) paying Zakaah, (4) fasting during Ramadhaan, and (5) performing Hajj to the Sacred House of Allaah—if one is able.

This can be summarized into two principles, that of creed and that of law.

**The Principle of Creed**

The core of this principle is the open testimony that there is no god but Allaah and that Muhammad is the Messenger of Allaah.

Regarding "there is no god", we mentioned above that the word ilah [god] in Arabic has more than 21 meanings, condensed to two ends: (1) the highest level of love and (2) the supreme show of obedience with full submission. Both achieve absolute servitude, about which Allaah Says (what means): *{I did not create jinn and man except to serve Me (in worship).}* (Quran, 51:56)

This servitude means obedience, complete compliance with the command of Allaah, and leading a productive life according to Allaah's way. *{Say: Verily My prayer, my sacrifice, my life, and my death belong to Allaah, Lord of the worlds.}* (Quran, 6:162)

In order to realize this significance and the great goals ahead, we must live our lives by accepting six beliefs—referred to as the pillars of faith in Sharee'ah terminology—which are to believe in (1) Allaah, (2) His Angels, (3) His Books, (4) His Messengers, (5) the last day, and (6) fate, whether good or bad.

Our preceding discussion throughout this book included various evidences that Allaah is The Providing Creator and the sole disposer of the affairs of this universe.

Likewise, true acceptance is by realizing that He is to be worshiped and obeyed, and that what He wants must be achieved in every affair of one's life, whether in belief, law, manners, morals or lifestyle.

One must also honor our Lord through His numerous names, submitting to the meanings thereof and seeking His assistance thereby. He Says (what means): *{The most beautiful names belong to Allaah, so call on Him therewith; and abandon those who deviate in His Names. They shall be repaid for what they have done.}* (Quran, 7:180)

**The Principle of Sharee'ah**

This is a foundation formulated by five essentials, without which no terrestrial society can lead lofty lives and taste the distinction of dignity—which Allaah wanted for them. These foundations are the preservation of what is dearest to people:

## Preservation of Religion

Religion is a human essential. If one does not serve his Lord in worship, he will serve something else. Our Messenger Muhammad, sallallaahu 'alayhi wa sallam, alluded to this when he said, *"The most beloved of your names to Allaah are 'Abd Allaah [slave of Allaah] and 'Abd ar-Rahmaan [slave of the Gracious]."* [Muslim]

## Preservation of the Body

The human body is a structure which Allaah built and bounded with honor. The Prophet, sallallaahu 'alayhi wa sallam, said, *"The end of the world and all it contains is easier in the Sight of Allaah than the murder of a single Muslim."* (At-Tirmithi: 1395, an-Nasaa'i: 3987)

## Preservation of the Mind

The mind is a gift from Allaah, by which He distinguished man from other animals. He honored him therewith and made it a sign of dignity and trust, just as He commanded him to preserve it. This is enacted in two ways: (1) by keeping it safe from the corruption of intoxicants and (2) by guarding it from something much worse: destructive doubt and suspicion, which are the weapons of the wicked who plot against this religion. However, as soon as those doubts and suspicions are challenged by the facts of religion, they collapse and vanish beneath the blazing light of revelation, known to those of knowledge.

## Preservation of Wealth

Wealth is the mainstay and true vitality of life. Through it progress is produced and civilization is constructed. Allaah has Facilitated it to satisfy the nation's needs. This requires us to implement the legislations of Allaah in the three matters of (1) gain, (2) growth and (3) consumption.

## Preservation of Lineage

It has become one of the most important objectives of Sharee'ah given that Islam regards the preservation of honor and family as the core of a righteous society. This is in contrast to corrupting man, seeking to sabotage him by calling him to doubtful matters which lead to the ruin of familial relations and the subversion of societies.

## What are the fruits of faith?

After careful consideration, one cannot conclude that there is anything or anyone more benefiting in this life, whether to an individual, a family, or an entire population, than the one able to freely furnish every form of favor. That is Allaah. He Says (what means): *{Whatever blessing you have, it is from Allaah.}* (Quran, 16:53) Allaah has already paved the path, but one must have faith to follow it. Regarding such favors, consider the following:

Abundant Provision

*{If they stayed the course, We would have quenched them with abundant water.}* [Quran: 72:16]

Support

*{It is upon Us that We support the believers.}* [Quran, 30:47]

Honor

*{But honor belongs to Allaah, the messenger, and the believers.}* (Quran, 63:8)

## Establishment on Earth

*{Allaah has promised those who believe and do righteous deeds that He will make them as successors in the earth, just as He made those before them as successors; and that He will establish for them their religion, which He has approved for them; and that He will replace their prior fear with security. "They serve Me. They associate no partner with Me."}* (Quran, 24:55)

## The Good Life

*{Whoever does righteous work—whether male or female—and is a believer, to such We shall give a good life; and We shall pay them their reward according to the best of what they used to do.}* (Quran, 16:97)

## Personal and Social Security

*{Those who believe and do not obscure their belief with wrongdoing, they shall have security; and they are the guided.}* [Quran, 6:82]

## Divine Guarantee to Sons and Daughters after Death

Regarding a story in which Allaah Preserves the inheritance of two children, the reason given being that *{their father was righteous.}* [Quran 18:82]

## Love

*{Verily those who believe and work righteous deeds, the Most Merciful will appoint for them affection.}* [Quran 19:96]

## Relationship to the Supreme Assembly of Angels

This relationship raises man from the dismay of clay to the elevation of the uplifted spirit, attached to its Lord. Regarding the angels who glorify His divinity, Allaah Says (what means): *{They seek forgiveness for those who believe, while saying, "Our Lord! You have encompassed everything in mercy and knowledge}* [Quran 40:7]

This is the path that will lead whoever follows it to achieving good fortune in this life and Paradise in the next.

We humbly ask Allaah to grant success and soundness of mind; to make our works solely for the Sake of His pleasure; that He makes of this book a lamp by which people are guided; that He shows us the truth as true and aids us to adhere to it; and that He shows us falsehood as false and aids us to avoid it.

May the peace and blessing of Allaah be upon our master Muhammad ibn 'Abdullaah Al-Haashimi, his family, and his Companions.

And the last of our call is "Praise be to Allaah, Lord of the worlds".

Printed by Libri Plureos GmbH in Hamburg, Germany